THE NOT SO SECRET GUIDE TO INSURANCE SALES

Real Advice. Proven Results. Old School Wisdom for the Modern Agent.

By Steven R. Wiatrek

The Not So Secret Guide to Insurance Sales
© 2025 Steven Wiatrek

ISBN: 979-8-218-86111-7

Published by The Wiatrek Group, LLC
Poth, Texas, USA

This book represents the personal opinions, experiences, and observations of the author. It is not intended as legal, financial, or professional advice. The views expressed are solely those of the author and do not reflect those of any past, present, or future employer, business partner, or affiliate.

Printed in the United States of America
First Edition – 2025

DEDICATION

To the agents, mentors, and friends who became my foundation.

To the ones who pushed, guided, and believed often more than I believed in myself.

This book is not just my story; it is a reflection of the countless hands that helped lift me along the way.

You may not be named here, but your impact is written into every page.

"Tomorrow is the day when the weak become strong.
I am not weak.
Tomorrow is the day when the failure will succeed.
I am not a failure."

— Og Mandino

Author's Note – Why I Wrote This Book

This book did not begin as a plan. It began as a season.

Not long ago, I stepped away from the captive insurance world feeling lost and uncertain. I didn't know if this industry still had room for people who believed in loyalty, faith, and the power of a handshake. I questioned almost everything—except my commitment to serve others.

Then Neil called.

He invited me to join the organization I'm with today. What I found wasn't just a team—it was a partnership of like-minded people who believed what I believed. They valued faith, community, and treating clients like neighbors, not transactions.

Over time, I began sharing my story. I spoke with new agents, struggling producers, and people who just needed encouragement. I didn't think my words mattered—until I realized they were making a difference. That's when I understood something clearly:

This book wasn't a decision. It was a calling.

This is not a manual. It is a message. A message about hope, integrity, and the belief that old-fashioned values still build world-class businesses.

So as you read this book—don't skim it. Take notes. Mark the margins. Let these pages challenge you, encourage you, and maybe even remind you of who you really are.

And maybe, together, we can build a grassroots movement—
A movement of faith over fear.
Service over sales.

Abundance over scarcity
A season of plenty.

— Steven Wiatrek

The Wiatrek Group Way

A Philosophy of Faith, Service, and Legacy in Insurance

The Wiatrek Group Way isn't a business model—it's a standard. It is the belief that insurance is more than policies and premiums. It is people, promises, and protection. It is serving families like they are your own. It is building something today that still matters tomorrow.

The Core Principles of the Wiatrek Group Way:

1. Faith Over Fear – Trust God, do what is right, and let integrity guide every decision.
2. Service Before Sales – We don't chase numbers; we care for people. The commissions follow the compassion.
3. Legacy Over Quotas – Success is not what you earn. It's what you build and who you become while building it.
4. Community Over Competition – We are not lone wolves. We're neighbors, partners, and protectors of our towns.
5. Excellence in the Small Things – Show up on time, return every call, shake every hand. Greatness is built in the ordinary.
6. Privacy, Respect & Presence – When a client walks into our office, their story matters. Phones go in the drawer. Doors close. Respect is non-negotiable.
7. Service Doesn't Stop at the Front Desk – You greet your client up front, walk them to your office, and when it's over—you walk them back, thank them, and remind them they matter.

This is who we are. This is how we work.

This is the Wiatrek Group Way.

TABLE OF CONTENTS

Chapter 1: The Myth of the Secret Weapon and Building Your Brand

Chapter 2: Building a Personal Brand & Selling Yourself

Chapter 3: Prospecting — The Lifeblood of Your Business

Chapter 4: Presentation & Closing Power

Chapter 5: The Freeze Moment

Chapter 6: Building Long -Term Clients

Chapter 7: Beginning with Client Experience

INTRODUCTION – FROM ONE AGENT TO ANOTHER

This book isn't a high-pressure sales manual or a hollow pep talk. It's a playbook written from real dirt roads, kitchen tables, late-night claims calls, and years of handshakes, smiles, and mistakes made along the way. It's written by someone who's been in the trenches — who's tasted both failure and success — not someone who's only ever spoken from a stage.

Insurance isn't just a product.

It's protection.

It's trust.

It's your word.

Every policy you write is a promise — that when life goes sideways, you'll be there to help pick up the pieces. That's the business we are truly in.

I didn't build my agency on fancy internet leads or slick scripts. I built it on relationships — real, lasting relationships with people in my community. My neighbors. Business owners. Teachers. Families. People I bump into at the grocery store, football games, and church parking lots. And here's the truth: people don't just buy insurance — they buy you.

That's why this book starts with mindset before it ever gets to sales techniques or closing scripts. Because if you know how to show up for people — how to make them feel seen, heard, and respected — the mechanics of sales take care of themselves.

What This Book Will Teach You

This book walks you through the journey of building and scaling a successful insurance career and agency:

- How to build your foundation on trust and service — not pressure or gimmicks.
- How to prospect smart, not desperate.
- How to close confidently without making people feel "sold."
- How to create loyalty so strong your clients defend you against competitors.
- How to become the name in your community — not just another agent.
- And how to leave behind more than a book of business — a legacy.

I'm going to share the real strategies, stories, and philosophies that turned walk-ins into lifelong clients and everyday moments into prospecting opportunities. Some are old school. Some are unique. All of them work — because they're rooted in something timeless: genuine human connection.

What I Ask of You

As you read, don't just memorize lines or techniques. Absorb the philosophy behind them. Understand the why, not just the how. Because at the end of the day:

- A handshake is more powerful than a script.
- A smile opens more doors than a pitch.
- A good name in your community is worth more than any marketing budget

This industry has room for every kind of agent — captive, independent, seasoned, or brand new. This book honors all paths.

I'm not here to argue which model is better. I'm here to tell you what worked for me — and what might work for you.
From one agent to another

"Success is not in what you have, but who you are"

-   Zig Ziglar

CHAPTER 1: The Myth of the Secret Weapon and Building Your Brand

When I first started out in the insurance industry, I was like so many other wide-eyed agents—hungry, determined, and desperate to prove myself. I had left the comfort of a fraternal life-insurance call center, where I spent four years taking inbound calls. I was proud of how far I had come, but I also felt like I was standing at the base of a mountain I didn't quite know how to climb. It was like trying to drink from a fire hose. Still, I was ready to make my mark.

Back then, I believed that if I could just find the right system— the right magic bullet—the right secret weapon—then I could skip the struggle. I thought success was something you could buy. I told myself that if I purchased the right course, the right leads, or the right sales script, everything would fall into place. Clients would line up, the phone would ring off the hook, and my career would take off.

I was sorely mistaken.

The myth of the secret weapon started small. One day, a colleague pulled me aside and whispered about a "lead program" that was supposed to change everything. It was exclusive, guaranteed, and proven. I was young, eager, and ready to believe. So I paid more than I should have and waited for the phone to ring. And ring it did—but on the other end were the same names every other agent in the district had already called three times that week. People were angry, frustrated, and tired of insurance calls. I didn't get a secret weapon. I got a lesson.

But like many young agents, I didn't learn it the first time. I thought maybe I'd just bought the wrong program. So I tried another. And another. Postcard campaigns promising "fifty guaranteed appointments a month." CRM systems that claimed to "automate prospecting." Scripts labeled "proven closers."

Each time, I told myself this one's it. And each time, I ended up frustrated and disappointed.

I learned the hard way that most so-called secret weapons aren't built to make you successful—they're built to make someone else rich off your hunger and hope.

The Captive Years

As a captive agent, I had structure—but I also had pressure. My company gave me a quota, a book of business I didn't own, and a script I was expected to follow. "Sell the products we want. Stick to the format." And whenever I struggled, the advice was always the same: Sell more. Buy more leads. Follow the script better.

For a while, I believed that was the only way. But after a few years, I began noticing something. The top producers—the ones winning trips and earning recognition—weren't relying on fancy programs. They were building something deeper: trust, relationships, and a brand.

That realization changed everything.

Why Agents Fall for the Scam

New agents are easy prey for these programs because they're desperate to succeed. It's like buying a lottery ticket—you know the odds are terrible, but hope whispers that maybe, just maybe, this one will hit. I know because I was one of them.

You're standing on shaky ground, trying to prove that you made the right career choice. So when someone comes along promising shortcuts, it's easy to listen. Hope is intoxicating, and once you're hooked, it's hard to stop chasing it.

But here's the truth that most of us learn too late: there are no shortcuts. You can't outsource trust. You can't automate your reputation. You can't pay someone else to make your name mean something.

I spent thousands chasing what could only be built the old-fashioned way—through handshakes, conversations, and consistency. The "secret weapon" wasn't something to find. It was something to become.

Ride for Your Brand

Cowboys of the past didn't ride for every herd—they rode for one brand, the one they believed in. Their loyalty was their honor, and their word was their bond.

Today, our brand isn't burned into hide—it's etched into our reputation. It's your name. It's how people talk about you when you're not in the room.

One of the most powerful moments in this business is when your name speaks for you before you even walk through the door.

Picture this: you're at a local fundraiser or Chamber of Commerce event. You're chatting with a friend when the mayor waves you over. "There's someone I want you to meet," she says, leading you across the room to one of the county's most respected business owners. Before you can even introduce yourself, he jumps up, shakes your hand, and says with a grin,

"Oh wow, mayor—how do you know my insurance agent and good friend?"

That's brand power money can't buy.

That's what happens when your reputation becomes bigger than your business card—when your community doesn't just recognize your name but trusts it, speaks it, and proudly connects themselves to it.

So ride for your brand like those cowboys did—with loyalty and pride. Defend it. Honor it. Let your actions speak so loudly that people already know who you are before you say a word.

Because when your brand is strong, your name needs no introduction.

KNOW YOUR WORTH

In this business, you're told, "You're only as good as your last week." Every Monday feels like a reset. No one cares about last month's numbers—only what you're doing right now. That pressure is real.

Insurance isn't a straight climb—it's hills and valleys. You'll have seasons where everything clicks—calls, referrals, renewals, success everywhere you turn. And then come the ruts—silence, doubt, rejection, and rate increases you can't control.

If you're not careful, you'll start to believe your worth rises and falls with the numbers.

That's why you need anchors—reminders of who you are beyond production reports.

For me, it started with a simple notebook—my Journal of Success. Every thank-you card, kind word, client compliment—I write it down or tuck it in. When the valley comes—and it will—I open it, and I remember: I make a difference. I matter.

Then there's my Wall of Fame. Not trophies—moments. Photos from community events, handwritten notes, newspaper clippings, pictures with clients I now call friends. It's not vanity—it's perspective.

Because the world will try to measure you by numbers. But numbers don't tell the whole story.

You are not your last commission check.

You are not your toughest week.

You are the promise you keep to your clients.

So when the phones are quiet and doubt creeps in—stand firm. Storms pass. Seasons change.

Know your worth. Guard it. Believe it.

Because the strongest thing you'll ever build in this business isn't your book.

It's your resilience.

Birds of a Feather: Who You Surround Yourself With Matters

Have you ever heard the phrase, "Birds of a feather flock together"? In this industry, it isn't just a cute saying—it's a truth worth paying attention to.

The next time you're at a corporate meeting, conference, or district gathering, take a moment to observe something most people miss: agents naturally group themselves by mindset and performance. Top producers sit with other top producers. Struggling agents sit with other struggling agents. Winners talk vision, strategy, and growth. Complainers talk about why things don't work.

I learned this lesson early.
At one of my first district meetings, I didn't know a soul and was about to sit just anywhere. My manager stopped me. He nodded toward a table and said quietly, "Don't sit there. Those agents are stuck in a pity party. They're drowning, but they don't want help—they want company. Attitude is contagious. Go sit with the winners."

So I did.

At that table, I didn't hear excuses—I heard solutions. They discussed marketing ideas, community networking strategies, and closing techniques that actually worked. I learned more by sitting quietly with those producers than I did from the entire presentation that day.

From then on, I made it a rule: always sit with the best. Even before I was one of them.

And something interesting happened... people started to associate me with the winners long before my numbers reflected it. My brand grew not just because I was producing, but because I was positioning myself in rooms where growth happened.

Success Lesson:

- Success is proximity—who you sit with, who you listen to, whose behavior you unconsciously mirror.
- Winners don't just share ideas—they transfer belief.
- You rise or sink to the standard of the people at your table.

Even today, whether it's a seminar, a mastermind, or a local Chamber of Commerce breakfast, I still look for someone who is further ahead than me—and I sit with them. Not out of pride, but out of purpose.

Because growth is rarely comfortable… but it is always intentional.

Do What Others Won't

If you want to build a book of business that lasts decades—not months—you must be willing to do what other agents refuse to do.

Anyone can send a quote by email or auto-generate a renewal letter. But not everyone will:

- Drive across town to hand-deliver an ID card to an elderly client.
- Personally pick up a payment from a customer who can't make it to the office.
- Show up on-site to walk a business owner through their commercial policy, face-to-face.

These things don't show up on a sales report… but they show up in people's hearts.

And hearts are where referrals are born.

I've learned something powerful over the years—people talk. That elderly client? She has children, grandchildren, neighbors, and friends at church. And when she tells them, "My agent took care of me," that's a better marketing campaign than any Facebook ad.

People don't remember the policy. They remember how you made them feel.

Brand Loyalty & Reputation

Your brand is not your logo. It's not your agency name.
Your brand is your behavior when no one is watching.

It's the way people talk about you when you leave the room. It's the trust your name carries at the local bank, school, church, or diner.

Real brand loyalty is when a client sticks with you—not because you're the cheapest—but because you're worth it.

Standing Out in a Crowded Field

Thousands of people sell insurance. Only a few become the name in their community.

The reason?
They don't try to be everywhere—they choose to be deeply rooted somewhere.

They:

- Shake hands and look people in the eye.
- Show up when it's inconvenient.
- Treat every client like a neighbor—not a number.

I call it The Good Ole Boy Approach. Simple. Honest. Unforgettable.
That's how legacies are built. Not through ads. Through actions.

Scam Spotting 101

For the new agents—let me save you some time, money, and heartbreak.

If a program:

- Promises overnight success—walk away.
- Says you'll never have to prospect again—run.
- Costs more than it teaches—it's not an investment, it's bait.
- Uses fear, hype, or urgency—it's for your wallet, not your well-being.

Most of these so-called "secret weapons" aren't built to make you successful. They're built to profit from your desperation.

Build Your Own Weapon

There is no magic formula—you are the formula.

Your handshake.
Your word.
Your integrity.
Your consistency.
Your decision to show up when others stay home.

These are the things no one can sell you—and no one can take from you.

Final Thoughts on Chapter One

This is why I chose to open this book with truth before tactics.

Because if you understand this—really understand it—every other chapter will make sense. The scripts, the closes, the systems, the marketing… they only work when the foundation is solid.

And that foundation is you.

You are the brand.
You are the neighbor people trust.
You are the calm voice when someone calls and says, "We lost everything in the fire—what do we do?"

So ride for your brand.
Because nobody else can ride it like you.

"Whatever you do, work at it with all your heart, as working for the Lord, not for men"
-    *Colossians 3:23*

CHAPTER 2: Building a Personal Brand & Selling Yourself

Let's get something straight from the start — the hard truth of sales:

Just because you got your insurance license doesn't mean people are going to line up at your door. They're not sitting at home waiting for a "new agent" to swoop in and save the day. They're busy living their lives, paying their bills, raising families, and solving problems you know nothing about.

You may feel proud to have passed your test — and you should — but the world doesn't suddenly see you as an expert. You must make them see it.
You must sell yourself before you can sell them anything else.

Why Branding Matters More Than Your License

When I first started, I made the same mistake most new agents make. I assumed friends and family would support me, that referrals would naturally start coming in, and business would just "happen." But the truth hit me hard — no one cares that you sell insurance… until you give them a reason to.

Your personal brand is that reason.

Your brand is not your agency's name, your logo, or your business card.

Your brand is:

- The way people feel when they hear your name.

- The reputation that follows you into rooms you haven't even walked into yet.
- The quiet conversations people have about you when you're not around.

And you don't build that in a day. You build it one handshake, one favor, one act of genuine service at a time.

How to Sell Yourself (Without Being Salesy)

Branding isn't about showing off — it's about showing up.
It starts with the little things:

- Dress like someone who represents something bigger than themselves.
- Speak with confidence — not arrogance.
- Be the same person in public as you are in private.

I always tell new agents:
"Wear your brand proudly, not loudly."
If you're at the grocery store — wear your agency shirt.
At your child's baseball game — wear your hat, cheer loudly, shake hands. Be involved.

But don't stop there.

Go to church. Join the men's or women's club. Volunteer. Coach. Serve food at local fundraisers. Be present at city council meetings, school board events, and chamber gatherings. People don't do business with the best agent — they do business with the agent they know, like, and trust.

Doing What Others Won't

Most agents think branding is just slapping a logo on a banner.
That's background noise.
You want to be unforgettable? Do something human.

When my oldest son joined T-ball, I didn't just sponsor the team.
I bought every child in his grade the book The Little Teammate
by Alan Williams. I wrote a personal message inside each one
reminding them they are loved, valued, and should always give
their best. With the school's permission, I read it to their classes
and took a photo with them for the local paper.

That one act did more for my reputation than any billboard ever
could.

To this day, teachers still read that same book every spring — the
one with my handwritten note inside.

Branding isn't a banner.
It's a memory.
It's the feeling you leave behind.

Community Presence (Without Bragging or Begging)

If you want to serve your community — don't post selfies about
it every five minutes. And don't hide in the back just to say you
"volunteered."

Be where the people are.

- Wear your branded cap or polo.
- Stand at the front, serving plates to the elderly.
- Carry trays to cars.
- Smile. Shake hands.

- Look people in the eye when you thank them for being there.

You want people to say:
"I always see him helping. He's everywhere. And he's genuine."

True Story — The Chicken Dinner That Built My Agency

When I left the captive world and opened my own brokerage, the first big event I attended wasn't a networking luncheon or business expo.

It was our Volunteer Fire Department's annual chicken plate fundraiser.

I showed up before sunrise with an apron and my agency shirt — not to hand out business cards, but to hand out barbecue plates. I poured sauce cups, stacked bags, wiped tables — whatever was needed.

And then something happened…

Old clients — people I had served years before — started coming up to me. They didn't know I had left the captive agency. They hadn't found anyone who served them like I did. They missed the personal phone calls. The help on bad days. The way I treated them like neighbors, not policy numbers.

I didn't give them a sales pitch. I just told them the truth:

"I outgrew where I was. I started my own agency. If you ever need me — I'm here."

Then I handed them my card and went back to serving plates.

I thought that was the end of it.
It wasn't.

They started telling other people standing in line.
"This is the guy who actually helped us. He answered the phone."
By noon, I had handed out every card I brought… twice.

That day taught me:

People don't remember advertisements. They remember
  presence.
Show up for your community… and your community will show
  up for you.

The Ripple Effect of Showing Up

Presence is powerful — especially when it's genuine.

What happened that day at the fire department wasn't luck or clever salesmanship. It was the result of years of quietly doing the right thing. When people see you serve, without asking for anything in return, they don't just remember — they talk.

That's the ripple effect of branding done right.

It's not the chicken plates. It's not the barbecue sauce cups. It's the message people walk away with:

"If he'll show up here when no one is watching, he'll show up when I need him."

Even months later, people stopped by my office or called the agency to say:

"I saw you at the chicken dinner… I've been meaning to reach out."

Not because I sold them anything. But because I was there.

Doing More Than "Showing Up" — Becoming A Fixture

Branding isn't built in a weekend — it's built in repetition.

If you show up once, people notice.
If you show up twice, people remember.
If you show up every time — people expect it.

That's when you've become part of the fabric of your town.

I made a decision early in my independent career:
If my community was gathering — I'd be there.

Not as "the insurance guy."
As a neighbor. A servant. A familiar face they trusted.

Practical Lessons You Can Use Right Now

1. Presence Over Pitch
People can smell a salesman from across the parking lot. But they
can also recognize sincerity. If you're volunteering, volunteer
because you care — not because there are potential clients in the
room.

2. Let Your Reputation Speak First
The most powerful marketing in the world is someone else
speaking your name in a room you're not in.

3. Familiarity Builds Trust
In small towns and counties, a familiar face beats the best digital
ad campaign.

4. Visibility ≠ Vanity
Don't post selfies every time you hand out a hamburger. The goal
is to be seen working — not seen taking credit.

5. Authenticity Lasts Longer Than Advertising
People don't expect perfection. They expect honesty.

Expanding Your Presence with Intention

Volunteering shouldn't just be random acts of kindness — it can be a thoughtful, meaningful strategy if done with the right heart. Here's how to scale it without losing authenticity:

• Choose 2–3 annual community events you will always support.
• Show up early — the relationships are built before the crowds arrive.
• Wear your brand — not as a costume, but as a quiet promise of reliability.
• Bring your team or family if possible — it humanizes your agency.
• Never make it about sales — if someone asks for your card, give it. If not, keep serving.

Why This Works

Because people don't want another agent.
They want their agent.
Someone they see in the grocery store, at the football game, at the fundraiser.
Someone who remembers their kid's name, their business, their story.

You're not just selling policies — you're earning trust.
And trust is built where few agents are willing to go:
• Behind the tables.
• In the kitchens.
• On the ball fields.
• At 6 a.m. with coffee and work gloves.

From Reputation to Opportunity

What happened at the Fire Department fundraiser wasn't luck —
it was a lesson.
People don't follow agents. They follow character, consistency,
and presence.
Your brand is not built when someone signs a policy — it's built
when they're watching you, when they're deciding if your name
is one they can trust with their home, family, and future.

That same principle is what turned my early community
involvement into actual business. Not by selling — but simply by
showing up.

Why Branding Is Built Long Before the Sale

Your brand is working even when you're not in the room.
If people can say these three things about you, you're winning:

- "I see him everywhere — and he's always helping
someone."
- "She's not just selling — she's serving."
- "If something goes wrong, I know I can call them."

That's branding. Not fonts, not logos — reputation in motion.

The Ripple Effect of Being Seen

When you show up in your community, you're planting seeds.
And like seeds, some take days, some take months, some take
years — but they grow.
Someone might not need insurance today, but when they do,
they'll remember:

- You helped carry meals to cars in the summer heat.

24

- You handed out water bottles at the parade instead of flyers.
- You showed up before sunrise to volunteer — and stayed until the cleanup.

That stays with people far longer than a Facebook ad.

Long-Term Visibility Strategy

This isn't a one-time act — it's a lifestyle.

Here's what consistency looks like in action:

- Choose 2–3 community events every year and commit to them — no matter how busy you are.
- Sponsor with purpose. Don't just pay to put your name on a banner — be physically present.
- Bring your team. When your agents serve beside you, it builds culture and multiplies visibility.
- Build relationships with event organizers. They're often the gatekeepers to every referral circle in town.
- Show up early. Stay late. The real conversations—the ones that build trust—happen before the crowds and after the applause.

Networking the Right Way (Not the Awkward Way)

Networking is not handing out business cards like confetti. True networking is partnership.
Stop chasing transactions — start building alliances.

The question isn't:
"Can you send me clients?"
It's:
"How can I make your life easier?"

The moment people realize you're not there to take — but to help — the doors open.

Power Partnerships That Built My Business

1. Realtors — "The On-Retainer Approach"

I built trust with realtors the same way I built it with clients: by showing up and doing what others wouldn't.

- I didn't cold-call — I brought coffee, shook hands, and said, "I'm here to make your closings smoother."
- I gave them two business cards:

    o   One with my office number + referral bonus
    o   One with my personal cell for after-hours closings

- I turned quotes around in hours — not days.
- I stayed for their sales meetings, not to speak — but to support.

Soon, I wasn't "an insurance guy."
I was their insurance guy. The one they trusted to help their clients close on time.

2. Loan Officers — Making Them Look Like Heroes

Loan officers don't care about your agency. They care about one thing: getting the deal funded without delays.
So, I made it my mission to be the fastest problem-solver in the process.

- Immediate quotes.
- Same-day binders.
- No surprises. No excuses.

If you remove stress from their process — you become part of their process.

3. Auto Dealerships — The Two-Card System That Never Fails

Car buyers need insurance before they can leave the lot.

So, I made it easy:

- One business card (office line, referral bonus).
- One card (personal cell — anytime, even weekends).
- Both rang to my phone — but the second one told them I was serious about helping their clients drive off that day.

And it worked. Dealerships began sending 5–10 deals a week.

Why This Works

You're not begging for business — you're earning trust.
You're not advertising — you're aligning with people who already influence buyers.
You're not chasing leads — you're becoming the answer before they even ask the question.

Prospecting Without Pressure — The Art of Being Remembered

Prospecting isn't about scripts or clever one-liners. It's about presence.
Not aggressive… not passive… but present.

Some of the best business I've ever written didn't come from cold calls or email blasts — it came from market days, farmers' markets, church festivals, county fairs, and small-town events.

Not because I sold anything.

But because I showed up as a neighbor, not a salesman.

The "No-Pressure Booth" Strategy

When I set up at local events, I don't come with a hard pitch. I come with:

A clean table
A small banner with my agency name
Ice-cold bottles of water
Fresh popcorn
A genuine smile and a handshake

No rate sheets.
No brochures shoved at people.
No "can I give you a quote today?"
Instead — I create a moment. A memory.
Think about it:
- A family walking through a hot Texas afternoon takes a free cold water and smiles.
- A kid grabs a bag of popcorn while his parents thank you.
- You talk about the weather, the game, the food truck down the road — not insurance.

And before they walk away, you simply hand them your card:

"Here's my card — if you ever need anything, I'm just a call away."

And they remember you.

Why This Works (When Others Don't)

- People hate being sold to — but they love being helped.
- You're not asking them for anything — you're giving them something.
- Their guard is down. Their trust goes up.
- You're no longer "an insurance agent." You're the guy who made them feel welcome.

Weeks later, months even — they call.

"Hey, I met you at the market — you gave me that bottle of water. Can I get a quote?"

That's not chance. That's strategy — human strategy.

How to Set Up a No-Pressure Booth (Simple but Effective)

Step	What You Do	Why It Works
1	Keep the table simple & clean	Less clutter = more approachability
2	Offer water, popcorn, lemonade or something refreshing	Hospitality creates connection
3	Wear your agency shirt or hat	Branding without bragging
4	Start conversations about life and not insurance	Relatability over persuasion
5	Hand the card naturally, not forcefully	"Here if you need me." Not "Call me now."
6	Smile. Shake hands. Make eye contact.	People remember how you made them feel

The Follow-Up Magic That Most Agents Miss

No-pressure doesn't mean no follow-up — it means respectful follow-up.

If someone signs up for a drawing, gives contact info, or says:
"Hey, call me next week…"
— you honor that.

Not with a sales pitch — but with sincerity:

"Hey John, it was great meeting you at Market Days. Hope your daughter won her soccer game. Let me know if you'd still like me to look at your auto and home insurance like we talked about."

Personal. Light. Professional.

The Long Game — How Small Moments Become Legacy Clients

This is not instant gratification. It's sowing seeds for a harvest.

One bottle of water turns into:
A quote.
Which turns into a client.
Which turns into a family.
Which turns into referrals.
Which turns into a legacy.

That's how I built my agency — not by pressure… but by presence.

Networking Isn't Passing Out Cards — It's Passing On Value

Most agents think networking is showing up to an event, handing out business cards like poker chips, and hoping the phone rings.

That's not networking — that's desperation.

True networking is service. It's walking into a room and asking, "Who can I help?" instead of "Who can help me?"

When you shift your approach from taking to giving — people don't avoid you… they introduce you

The Power Partners You Need (And How to Earn Their Trust)

In this business, the right relationships can generate more leads than any Facebook ad or purchased list.

Here are the four partnerships that built my agency faster than anything else:

Partner Type	Why It Matters	What They Need	How You Win Them
Realtors	Every homebuyer needs insurance before closing.	Speed & reliability. No delays.	Be their "on-retainer insurance guy". Give quotes within hours, not days.
Loan Officers	A slow insurance agent can delay a loan.	Fast binders, clear communication.	Make them look like heroes to their clients.
CPAs	They know every business owner's budget and pain points.	Someone who can lower costs or increase deductions.	Save them or their clients money, they send everyone they know.
Auto Dealers	Every car sale needs proof of insurance immediately.	Fast action's especially after 5 PM.	Be available evenings & weekends. Help them close deals.

The "On-Retainer" Approach (Without Charging a Dime)

I used to tell realtors and lenders:

"Think of me like your attorney on retainer — except you don't have to pay me when you need me. I'm just one call away to help your deals close on time."

No pressure. No contracts. Just reliability.

They don't want someone who sells insurance — they want someone who solves problems.

Real Example — Saving a CPA, Gaining His Entire Client List

A CPA I met through a mutual friend didn't want to talk at first. He said, "I don't want to be sold."

I nodded and said, "Fair. How about I save you money instead?"

I offered to review his group health plan.

- He was overpaying by $10,000 a year.

- I added dental and vision coverage.

- His benefits got better. His bill got smaller.

He looked at me and said, "My clients need this."

And just like that — one conversation turned into dozens of commercial accounts.

Not because I pitched. Because I proved.

Auto Dealers & The Two-Card System

(One of the simplest referral strategies I still use today)

When I met finance managers at dealerships, I didn't ask for referrals. I gave them two cards:

1. Office Card — with my agency line and $25 referral bonus.

2. Personal Cell Card — for after-hours emergencies.

And I'd say:

"This one earns you a bonus during business hours.

This one gets your client on the road after 5 PM."

Nine times out of ten — they grab the second card.

Why? Because speed is money.

Truth? Both cards ring to my cell.

But the system positions me as professional and personal.

And it trains them to see me as someone they depend on — not just call when it's convenient.

Networking Rules That Built My Agency

Do this, and you'll never chase leads again:

Never lead with "Can you send me referrals?"

Lead with "How can I help your clients and make your life easier?"

Ask more questions than you answer.

Take notes. Follow up. Do what you say you'll do — fast.

Be present at their events — not just your own.

Become their "insurance guy." Not just an insurance guy.

Practical Lessons from a Simple Volunteer Event

That volunteer fire department chicken dinner didn't just feed people — it fed my perspective. It taught me more about branding, service, and community than any sales conference or marketing course ever could. Looking back, there were powerful lessons hidden in that simple act of showing up, putting on an apron, and serving my neighbors.

Here are the truths I carried with me from that day forward:

• Presence Over Pitch

People can feel when you're there to serve versus when you're there to sell.

When you show up simply to help — without an agenda, without expectation — you earn something far more valuable than a lead… you earn trust.

• Let Your Reputation Speak Before You Do

Anybody can say, "I care about my clients."

But when clients say it about you — when they tell others how you showed up, how you helped, how you followed through — that carries weight no advertisement can buy.

• Familiarity Builds Loyalty

In small towns, tight communities, and rural counties, a familiar face is more valuable than a polished ad campaign.

When people see you — year after year — volunteering, serving, smiling, and showing up... you stop being "just another agent."

You become their agent.

• Visibility Doesn't Require a Stage

Too many agents believe visibility means setting up a booth, passing out flyers, and forcing a pitch.

Sometimes, the most powerful branding is done quietly:

- Holding the door for someone.

- Carrying plates to the elderly.

- Refilling tea and smiling like you're exactly where you want to be.

• Authenticity Always Wins

When someone asked me why I left the captive insurance world, I didn't give them a polished corporate answer.

I told them the truth: I outgrew where I was. I wanted to serve people better — my way.

People connect with real stories, not rehearsed scripts.

The Ripple Effect of Showing Up

Trust doesn't happen overnight. It's not built in a single conversation, appointment, or flyer.

It happens drop by drop — like rain filling a well.

That day, people didn't just remember that I was at the fundraiser…

They remembered that:

- I was there before the doors opened.

- I was wearing my agency shirt but serving with my hands, not my logo.

- I wasn't selling anything — I was simply present.

Weeks later, people called into my office saying:

"Hey, I saw you working the chicken lunch. I've been meaning to call you about insurance."

That's the ripple effect. One act of service, hundreds of quiet endorsements.

Expanding Your Volunteer Presence

Being present at one event is powerful. But being present consistently — that's how your community goes from recognizing your face… to trusting your name.

If you want your brand to grow roots, not just branches, here's how you expand your visibility with purpose — not noise.

How to Build Community Presence the Right Way

• Identify the Right Events — Not Just Any Events
Don't just show up anywhere there's a crowd.
Pick events that mean something to your people — and to you:

- Volunteer fire department fundraisers
- School festivals and FFA stock shows
- Church picnics and youth sports events

- Town parades, market days, livestock auctions

These aren't "business opportunities." These are relationship opportunities.

Most people think "networking" means handing out business cards like candy and begging people to send you leads.

That's not networking.
That's desperation.

Real networking isn't asking people to help you grow.
It's showing people how helping you also helps them — their business, their clients, and their reputation.

The Difference Between Networking and Begging

Begging says:
"Please give me leads."

Networking says:
"Here's how I can make your life easier and your clients happier."
People don't want to be your "lead source." They want to be your partner.

Partnership Over Prospecting

When you build relationships with professionals like:

- Realtors
- Mortgage loan officers
- Auto dealerships
- CPA's and tax professionals
- Bankers and commercial lenders

You're not chasing leads — you're creating pipelines.

And the secret is this:

They don't care about you writing policies.
They care about you solving their problems.

What Every Referral Partner Wants to Know

Before anyone sends you a client, they're asking themselves:

1. Will this make me look good — or bad?
2. Will my customers thank me — or complain about me?
3. Can I trust this person to follow through — fast?
4. Do they make my job easier — or harder?

If you can answer those questions with your actions — not just your words — you've earned a partner, not just a lead.

Case Study: How I Won Over a CPA (and His Entire Client List)

There was a local CPA who wouldn't give me the time of day. He told me up front — "I don't want to be sold anything."

So instead of selling, I offered value.

I told him:
"Give me a shot — one group health quote for your firm. No pressure. No commitment. Let me prove myself."

He agreed.

I ran the numbers.
I found a better plan.
I saved him $10,000 a year — and added dental and vision coverage.

He didn't just say thank you.
He said, "Where have you been? I need you to take care of my clients the way you took care of me."

That's networking.
Not because I asked for leads — but because I earned them.

The Realtor Strategy — Being "On Retainer" Without Charging a Penny

When I opened my independent agency, I was invited by Cristal to share her RE/MAX brokerage office.

I wasn't just available.
I was present.

Realtors would walk buyers over and say:
"This is Steven — he'll take care of your insurance before you leave here today."

Here's why it worked:

- I didn't pressure them — I partnered with them.
- I didn't act like a vendor — I acted like a teammate.
- I communicated every step of the way.
- I made closings easier, faster, and smoother.

So I started using a simple analogy they loved:
"Think of me like your attorney on retainer — except you don't pay me when you need me. But I'm always here."

They never forgot that.

The Power of Quiet Consistency

You don't build a personal brand in a weekend. You don't become the "go-to agent" in your town because of one viral social media post, one clever advertisement, or one great sales month.
You earn it — day after day — with consistency.
Not loud, flashy, look-at-me consistency.
Quiet consistency. The kind people notice even when you're not trying to be noticed.

It's showing up to the football game even when you're tired —
shaking hands, smiling, supporting the kids.
It's answering the phone when a client calls at 7:30 PM with a
question about a claim.
It's replying to texts, even when there's no commission attached.
It's the handwritten note after a big life event — a new baby,
graduation, a lost loved one.
It's the little things that no one applauds in public…
But everyone remembers in private.

Over time, that quiet consistency becomes your reputation.
People may not comment on it, but they talk about it when you're
not in the room:

"He always shows up."
"She never forgets us."
"He checks in even when he's not trying to sell something."

That is how your name becomes a brand — not through
billboards, but through trust.

FINAL THOUGHTS – CHAPTER 2

Your Name Is the Brand

If there's one thing you take from this chapter, let it be this:
People are not buying insurance — they're buying you.

Your logo might open a door. Your license might get you in the
game.
But your character — your consistency — is what makes people
stay.
You don't need to be the loudest agent.
You don't need the fanciest marketing.
You just need to do what most won't:

- Show up when it doesn't benefit you.

- Serve when no one is watching.
- Be the same person in the grocery store line as you are in the office.
- Let your actions advertise for you.

Because one day, without you even realizing it, your community will begin to do your marketing for you.
People will tag your name in social media threads:
"Who's a good insurance agent?"
And five people will reply, "Call Steven — he's the one who actually takes care of you."

That is branding.
Not noise.
Not hype.
Just trust — built one handshake at a time.

So keep showing up. Keep riding for your brand.
Because the greatest endorsement you will ever earn is not printed on a billboard —
It's spoken quietly when someone says,
"That's my agent — and I trust him."

"You don't build a business. You build people, and people build the business."

- *Zig Ziglar*

CHAPTER 3: Prospecting — The Lifeblood of Your Business

Why Prospecting Matters More Than Anything

Let's get one thing straight: if you want to survive and thrive in the insurance industry, you must master the art of prospecting. Prospecting isn't part-time. It's not something you do only when business is slow. It is the lifeblood of your agency. Every appointment, every policy, every renewal begins with a prospecting effort. Period.

Too many new agents imagine phones ringing off the hook the moment they get licensed. Real life doesn't work like that. No one is waiting on the edge of their seat for you to sell them insurance. You have to go meet people where they are.

The agents who build lasting businesses aren't the ones with the fanciest websites or biggest ad budgets. They're the ones who consistently put themselves in front of people. Every. Single. Day.

Selling the Appointment, Not the Product (V.R.P.O.C.)

Prospecting is about conversations, not closing. The number-one mistake new agents make is trying to sell the product on the first interaction. Your first goal is simple: sell the appointment. That's it. If you can get face-to-face (or Zoom-to-Zoom), your odds of success multiply.

I discovered the V.R.P.O.C. framework one night scrolling LinkedIn:

- V — Verify
- R — Re-verify
- P — Pitch
- O — Overcome Objections
- C — Close the Appointment

Example: Ring. Ring. Secretary answers. You're calm, confident, and polite. You ask for the person who manages insurance. You verify you're speaking to the decision-maker. Only then do you deliver your pitch:

"Hi, my name is Steven Wiatrek with the Wiatrek Group. I've helped businesses like yours lower insurance costs while improving coverage. I'd like to set a short meeting to show you how. Are you available Tuesday morning or Thursday afternoon?"

Notice: you're not quoting over the phone or dumping information. You're simply asking for an appointment.

Field Note: Don't sell policies on the call. Sell the right to meet.

Prospecting with Purpose

Never make a call without a purpose. Aimless calls sound like cold sales pitches. Purpose-driven calls open doors. "I think I can help your business" or "Want a quote?" is vague and easy to brush off. Create a reason to listen and a sense of urgency that makes the other person lean in.

COMMERCIAL LINES: THE GAP STRATEGY

After the front desk transfers me to the person in charge of insurance, I introduce myself clearly and confidently:

"My name is Steven Wiatrek. I'm an insurance consultant — and, if it's deemed necessary, I can place coverage. The reason for my call is that I believe there may be a serious gap in your current coverage that could leave your business vulnerable."

I don't open with "Can I give you a quote?" I open with a problem that deserves attention. I emphasize the potential gap and position myself as a problem-solver, not a salesperson.

This works because a very high percentage of commercial policies don't carry business interruption coverage. That stat is a leverage point. Even if I don't know for sure whether they have the gap, the likelihood is high enough to justify the meeting. Once I'm in, I often:

- Match price or come in lower
- Add business interruption to strengthen the plan
- Cross-sell employee benefits where appropriate

This isn't a gimmick. It's strategic positioning. I'm not another quote; I'm the consultant who protects them from what they don't see coming.

Field Note: Lead with a risk they care about. Earn the review before you earn the right to quote.

PERSONAL LINES: THE 30-DAY RENEWAL CALL

Personal lines is different, but just as purposeful. I don't call out of the blue — I call 30 days before renewal:

"Hi, I'm reaching out because it's time for our renewal appointment. We'll review pricing, check for any rate changes, and — most importantly — talk through any lifestyle changes that might affect your coverage."

People outgrow their coverage as their lives change. By calling before renewal, I'm a proactive advisor, not a reactive order-taker.

Why this approach works:

- Creates urgency: "Problem" or "review" language makes people listen
- Establishes authority: Consultant first, agent second
- Builds trust early: Sounds like partnership, not pitch
- Improves closing ratios: Groundwork is laid before the meeting

Every appointment starts with a call. It can sound like a telemarketer — or like a trusted advisor. The difference is purpose.

The Night Everything Changed: One Word — "Leverage"

"Call night" is when the whole agency stays late, orders pizza, and pounds the phones. One night, my manager Mark paused at my door while I fumbled through another dead-end call. He sat down, tapped the desk, flipped over my business card, and wrote one word: Leverage.

"Without a reason for the call — without leverage — they won't make time for you. People don't give up their evening because you want an appointment. They do it because you gave them a reason: a coverage gap, an opportunity, a renewal review, a personal touch. A purpose."

From that day forward, I stopped calling hoping for time and started calling with purpose. The numbers flipped. My calls didn't just fill a quota — they filled my calendar. I still keep that card on my desk.

Field Note: Leverage isn't pressure. It's clarity about what's at stake.

Leveraging Confidence, Rejection, and Mental Toughness

Mark didn't give me a magic line or shortcuts. He gave me perspective:

"Steven, people don't move unless they have a reason to. Your job isn't to pressure them — it's to give them a reason. That's leverage."

What leverage looks like in real life: It's not pressure. It's positioning.
Instead of, "Do you want to meet to go over your insurance?" try:

"Mr. Johnson, I know you're busy. But if something happened tonight, is your family protected the way you think they are? That's exactly what I want to help you with. Let's take 20 minutes and make sure your bases are covered."

That's leverage — responsibility turned into action, without fearmongering.

Rejection — the toll booth on the road to success: If rejection scares you, this business will eat you alive. People will ignore you, cancel, ghost, and delay. Rejection is not a verdict; it's a filter. It separates those who need you now from those who need you later. Mentally strong agents don't crumble after a "no." They nod, write it down, and move on.

Mental toughness — the difference maker: It's built by showing up on days you don't feel like it, making the extra call when pride says go home, and remembering your purpose is bigger than your feelings.

When I walked out of Mark's office that day, nothing around me had changed — but I had. I stopped begging for appointments and started creating reasons for them. I stopped letting rejection discourage me and treated it as confirmation that I was still in the fight.

Field Note #4: Leverage is not manipulation. It's reminding people of what matters — and giving them a reason to act now, not later.

Appointment Mastery — What You Do After "Yes"

Getting the appointment isn't victory; it's opportunity. "Leverage opens the door. Honor keeps you in the room."

How to show up like a professional — not a peddler:

- Before the appointment

    o Learn their name, spouse's name, business/family detail → Shows you see people, not prospects
    o Bring printed materials (not just a laptop) → People trust what they can hold
    o Dress one level higher than the client → Respect earns respect
    o Breathe, slow down, be present → Rushed minds don't build trust

How I open almost every appointment:

"Thank you for your time. Before we begin — what's the most important thing in your life that you want protected?"

Then I listen. That answer is their why. Once someone gives you their why, you're not selling a policy — you're protecting a story.

Field Note: You don't sell insurance in an appointment — you earn the right to protect someone's life.

The Flow of a Winning Appointment

1) The Entrance — Respect the moment.
Knock with confidence, not arrogance. Smile like you mean it. If you enter a home, ask if you should remove your shoes.

2) The Table — Don't start with business.
Connect first: "How long have you been in business?" "Is that your daughter's graduation photo?" Connection lowers walls.

3) Permission — Set the tone.

"Is it okay if I share how I help families and businesses? If it's a fit, great. If not, no hard feelings."

4) Ask before you answer.

"Before I make any recommendations — what's the one thing you never want taken from you?"

5) Take notes — by hand.
It signals care, presence, and stewardship.

6) Present only what matters.
Tie their fear to your solution: "You said you don't want your wife to worry about the house. Here's how we protect that."

7) Close softly, honestly.

"I'd be honored to take care of this for you. Would you like me to put this in place for your family?"

8) Leave better than you arrived.
Firm handshake. Sincere thanks. "You'll never have to chase me. I'll answer the phone."

Field Note: Make their table feel safe, and they'll invite you back — sometimes for life.

Handling Resistance with Grace — Not Pressure

You'll hear: "Let me think about it." "Can you email it?" "We're happy where we are." Resistance isn't rejection; it's hesitation — usually because they don't feel safe yet.

The calm response strategy:

1. **Agree, don't argue:**
   "I completely understand. Most people feel the same way at first — until they see how this actually protects what matters."
2. **Bring it back to their why:**
   "Earlier you said if something happened, you don't want your employees or family to suffer. That's exactly why I'm here."
3. **Remove pressure completely:**
   "Whether you do this with me or not, I want you fully informed. If it makes sense — great. If not, at least you'll know you made a wise decision."

The soft close:

"Would you like me to take care of this for you?"

If they're not ready:

"No problem. When would you feel comfortable revisiting it — and how can I make that easier?"

Field Note: The goal isn't to win the debate. The goal is to help them win their future.

When They Say "No" — Letting Go Without Losing the Relationship

Not every appointment ends with a signature. Early on, those moments crushed me — until I learned that "no" doesn't mean never; it often means "not yet." Your job isn't to force the door open; it's to make sure they remember who knocked with respect.
Story — the rancher who told me "no" three times:
Big spread, cattle, barns, loyal to his agent. I showed up, earned a hearing, and heard my first "no." I checked in twice a year — breakfast tacos, a Christmas calendar — never to sell; just to say hello. Second year: drought. "No" again. Third year: storm, barn roof collapsed, couldn't reach his agent. Two days later:
"Steven, are you still willing to help an old rancher who told you no three times?"

We rewrote everything. He became one of my most loyal clients — not because I pushed, but because I stayed.

How to walk away — the right way:

- Thank them sincerely
- Leave a card, not a presentation
- **Ask permission to check in at renewal:**
  "Would it be alright if I check in around renewal time? No pressure — just to see how things are going."
- Make the note — then keep the promise

Field Note: A "no" handled with grace opens more doors than a "yes" forced with pressure. "You catch more with honey than vinegar" as my Grandpa always said.

Follow-Up Without Becoming a Pest

Most agents lose business not because they're bad at selling —
but because they're bad at following up the right way. They
either don't follow up at all, or they follow up so aggressively
they burn trust.

"Follow-up isn't about chasing someone. It's about proving you
haven't forgotten them."

Rule: Follow up with respect. Be present, not painful.

My follow-up rhythm:
- They said "Call me in a week" → I call exactly when I
  said I would.
  "Just keeping my promise to check back with you."
- They said "Not interested right now" → I wait until
  renewal month or ~6 months.
  "No selling — just checking in like I said I would. How
  are things going?"
- They ignored my quote → I follow up once, then let it
  rest 3–6 months.
  "Hope you've been well. If anything changes, I'm here
  when you're ready."
- Good meeting, no decision → I send a handwritten thank-
  you card.
  "Thank you for your time. Whenever you're ready, I'll be
  here to protect what matters to you."

The "Breakup Method" — when they ghost you:
A fellow owner, Courtney, taught me this and I use it today:

"Hi ____, I haven't heard back from you, so I'm going to assume
this may not be the right fit right now. No worries at all. If
anything changes or you ever need help in the future, I'll still
be here."

No pressure. No guilt. A respectful close of the loop. Ironically,
this gets more replies than most follow-ups, because no one likes

being the one who walked away. And even if they don't respond, you still win — you protected your time and professionalism.

Story — the bakery owner:
Mother-daughter team. Loyal to a cousin. I bought a cinnamon roll, left a card, and said, "If you ever need a second opinion or your cousin retires, I'd be grateful for a call." I stopped by every few months, never pushed. Two years later: "Our cousin left the business. Mom said, 'Call the agent who never pressured us but never forgot us.'" That's follow-up done right.

Field Note: Follow-up isn't chasing people. It's reminding them — gently — that you're still here, and you still care.

Knowing When to Dismount: Letting Go of Dead Leads

We've all chased the "maybes," held onto "call me next week," and told ourselves those brush-offs mean we're close. Sometimes "maybe" really means no. Clinging to dead leads gives the illusion of productivity but robs you of real opportunity.

Simple script that saves dignity (and time):

"Mr./Ms. Prospect, I understand you want time to think and I'll follow up as requested. For your sanity — so I'm not a pushy salesman — and for mine — so I don't keep interrupting your evening — can we be frank? If you're not interested, please just tell me. I won't be offended, and I'll still be your friend and agent afterward."

As an independent owner, I have every producer keep a prospect spreadsheet (name, phone, each contact date). After three consistent follow-ups with no progress, they move the name to a Future List six months out. We don't lose the lead — we stop bleeding time.

Field Note: Letting go isn't giving up. It's creating space for your next yes.

The Power of "No"

"No" usually means "not right now." Track every contact. If they say no, ask for renewal and calendar it. Follow up on schedule.

Most agents stop after ten calls. When I started, I was one of them. Don't be most agents. Set a weekly goal for quotes or appointments and don't stop until you hit it. Sometimes 20 calls. Sometimes 50. The law of large numbers works — if you do.

Field Note: Treat every "no" like a "future yes" with a date attached.

Creative Prospecting Strategies

Phone work is vital — but top producers use a mix of tactics. The more natural touchpoints you create, the more likely you'll be remembered when insurance becomes urgent.

Some of my best business came from ordinary moments — standing in the grocery line, pumping gas, chatting at a café. Bring your business into everyday life without making it feel forced.

The Business Card Multiplier Effect

Never hand out one card. Hand out three. With one card, they keep it or toss it. With three, they keep one and share two. Use the back:

"Show this card when getting a quote for a chance to win our
  holiday giveaway."

Strategic Card Placement

Leave a few cards daily in high-traffic idle-time spots — grocery registers, gas pumps, coffee counters. Ten cards once won't change your business. A few cards every day for a year creates thousands of impressions.

Conversation Starter: The "SOL" Bracelet

A simple rubber bracelet — logo on one side, SOL on the other. People smirk and think "out of luck." I smile:

"Get your mind out of the gutter — SOL stands for Standard of
  Living. It's my reminder why I do what I do: to protect
  people's standard of living."

Why it works: it's personal, visible, and invites people to ask. Wear it daily, use light humor, tell the story with heart, carry cards, and be genuine.

Grocery Store Prospecting — "The Pickle Story"

My favorite strategy is grocery store prospecting. I'll "struggle" to find an item and ask with a grin:

"Hey, sorry — do you know where they hide the dill pickles? I'm convinced they're in witness protection."

People help. I thank them, hand a card: "If you ever need help with insurance, I'd be happy to return the favor." One day I gave two cards — to a shopper and an employee. A week later Deborah, my secretary got a call asking for "the pickle man." We laughed — and I gained a new client.

Everyday Prospecting: Restaurants & Personal Encounters

Restaurants are prospecting gold — people-driven, community-rooted. I choose sit-down spots when I can. I leave a cash tip with a handwritten note:

"Thank you for your kindness and great service. I appreciate you."

Staff remember. "Hey, you're the insurance guy." They introduce me to managers/owners.

Pickup order that landed a big account: I asked the clerk, "Who handles your restaurant's insurance?" He brought the owner. I reviewed, found gaps/overpriced coverages, and saved $6,000 annually. That account became a major referral source.

How to implement:
- Choose local spots
- Be consistent
- Leave cash tips + handwritten notes

- Ask, "Who handles the insurance here?"
- Be ready to talk
- Follow up gently

Expand beyond restaurants: salons, coffee shops, farmers' markets — anywhere people gather.

Make It a Routine

- Set a daily card goal (even 10 adds up)
- Target high-flow times/places
- Keep cards accessible (pocket, console, bag)
- Use humor and warmth
- Make it personal — a simple "thank you" moment is a perfect segue

Building long-term visibility: You're creating a web of small, meaningful interactions. One card today might turn into a policy months later.

Real-world ripple: I once handed out three cards at a coffee shop — one to the cashier, two to people in line. Months later a woman called: "My neighbor gave me your card. She got it from someone who got it at the coffee shop." That one moment turned into home, auto, life — and a referral to her brother-in-law's business.

When You're Tired of Hearing "No" — Prospecting Fatigue

Prospecting isn't hard because it requires skill. It's hard because it requires heart. Anybody can dial a phone. But to keep calling after the 20th "no" — that takes resilience.

A day I wanted to quit calling:
Thursday afternoon in my captive days. Thirty-seven calls by 3:00 p.m. — all declines, ignores, or "email me." I stared at the ceiling: "What's the point?" Mark walked by:

"How many calls today?"
"Thirty-seven."
"Good. Make thirty-eight."

Call #38 answered. Booked the appointment. Wrote the policy. Paid the mortgage that month.

What I learned:

- You don't need motivation to keep a commitment
- Discipline is doing the work after the feeling is gone
- The next call might change everything — if you make it

How I push through today:

- Set call goals, not time goals (talk to 20 people)
- Track progress, not just effort (conversations, not dials)
- Reset briefly (step outside, then return)
- Keep proof you're making an impact (thank-you notes, voicemails)

Field Note: Success isn't built on the first call. It's built on the one you make after you're tired of calling.

When the Pipeline Finally Hits — Don't Let Success Make You Soft

The week everything hit at once Monday morning. I walked in with a cold Diet Coke from Circle K, ready for prospecting calls. Before I touched the phone: a commercial request, a realtor referral, a long-chased business owner ready to review numbers. By noon, five appointments. By Wednesday, more quotes than the previous three weeks combined. By Friday, I was scrambling — non-stop calls, overflowing email, half-finished quotes, service tickets, kids' schedules. For the first time, my problem wasn't finding business — it was keeping up with it.

That night, alone in the office at 9:30 p.m., I stared at a stack of open quotes and thought: "I prayed for this... so why do I feel out of control?"

What went wrong?
I stopped doing what created the success.

No more morning prospecting.
No more time blocks.
No more planting seeds — just reacting.

The fix:

- Protect prospecting time again (even 30 minutes)
- Organize the madness (no more napkin quotes; track follow-ups, renewals, personal notes)
- Stop trying to be the entire agency (delegate service so you can keep selling)

It's easy to stay disciplined when business is slow; hunger keeps you focused. The real test is when you're finally busy — and comfort tempts you to relax on the habits that got you here.

Field Note: Success doesn't mean you stop planting seeds. It means you have more fields to harvest.

Final Thought — Chapter 3

Prospecting, rejection, appointments, follow-ups — even success itself — none of it is the real test.

The real test is whether you keep showing up.

Not just when people answer.
Not just when the quotes turn into policies.
But when it's quiet.
When the phone doesn't ring.
When you're tired of hearing "no."
Or when momentum finally hits and comfort tempts you to slow down.

This business is built in the unseen moments where nobody is clapping — and you choose to keep going anyway.

At the end of the day, insurance isn't about policies or premiums. It's about this:

You showed up. You cared. You didn't quit — on them, or on yourself.

"Faith is taking the first step even when you don't see the whole staircase."

\-   *Martin Luther King Jr.*

CHAPTER 4: Presentation & Closing Power

Where Trust Becomes Commitment

Presentations and closing are where good agents become unforgettable. Prospecting fills your calendar, but being face-to-face—sitting across a kitchen table or a conference desk—is where trust is earned, decisions are made, and families' futures quietly shift.

People don't buy insurance.
They buy confidence in the person across the table.

That's why your tone, your posture, your calmness, and your genuine intention matter far more than your rate sheet or brochure. Insurance isn't a transaction. It's stewardship. And in this chapter, you'll learn how to guide people—not pressure them—into decisions that protect what they love most.
Before I step out of my vehicle for any appointment, I pause, bow my head, and pray:

"Lord, help me serve this family well. Let me speak with honesty, listen with compassion, and guide them with integrity. Let me be Your servant in this work."

That prayer centres me. It reminds me that my job isn't to sell—it's to serve.

Why Presentation Matters More Than Product

A flawless quote won't save a poor presentation. But a strong presentation can redeem an average quote.
Your presentation isn't about flooding people with facts or flexing product knowledge. It's about:

- Telling a story rather than reciting data
- Making the invisible feel real—security, loss, legacy
- Helping them picture what life looks like with protection versus without it
- Making them feel safe, not sold

Og Mandino said, *"To bring peace, you must first carry it."*
If you walk into a room anxious, rushed, or unsure… that's what they'll feel. If you walk in calm, focused, and prepared—they'll trust you before you ever talk numbers.

The Power of Intentional Presence

Before you open your briefcase or click your laptop:

- Be early, never on time. My rule for my team is simple—"If you're on time, you're late."
- Greet with warmth, not formality. Smile. Say their name. Shake their hand like it means something.
- Scan the room. Family photos, sports memorabilia, kids' artwork—all of it tells a story.
- Sit beside them when possible—not across. This is a conversation, not a negotiation.
- Match their tone. If they're casual, be calm. If they're serious, be steady.

People decide whether they trust you before you ever open your folder.

Smooth Transitions — Especially Into Life Insurance

Most agents crash when they move from auto or home into life insurance—because it feels forced, like a pitch.

The best transitions sound like this:

"We've made sure your cars and home are protected. Now let's talk about something even more important—you. Because none of those things matter if the income that pays for them disappears."

Or:

"You told me your biggest priority is your family's future. Let me show you how we protect that—not with a policy, but with a plan."

Life insurance isn't a product—it's a love letter written in advance. When the conversation flows from their story, not your script, they lean in instead of backing away.

FIELD NOTE: "You don't earn the close by talking.
You earn it by making people feel seen, safe, and understood."

CLIENT-LED NEEDS ANALYSIS — LET THEM OWN THE NUMBERS

Most agents make one critical mistake: they tell clients what they need instead of helping them discover it themselves.

But when the client writes the numbers, they own the numbers.

That's why one of the most powerful tools in your presentation isn't a PowerPoint slide, a company brochure, or a polished script...

It's a simple sheet of paper and a pen.

Why the Client Must Fill Out the Form

When you hand a prospect a pen, and they begin to fill in their own debts, income, kids' names, and mortgage balance—something changes:

- They shift from being sold to → to taking responsibility.
- It stops being your idea → and becomes their reality.
- You're no longer convincing them of need → they're acknowledging their own need.

I always start this portion by writing their name at the top:

John & Sarah Thompson
Needs Analysis
Then I slide the paper toward them with a pen and say:

"Most people don't really know how much protection their family would need if something happened. Let's figure it out together. You fill it in, I'll guide you."

Then I go quiet.

Silence is powerful.
People naturally begin writing.
And once they write it—they believe it.

THE FLOW THAT MAKES IT WORK

The form must feel like a story—not a spreadsheet.
The steps I follow:
1. Final Expenses
2. Debt
3. Mortgage or Rent
4. Children's Education
5. Readjustment Income (Income Replacement)

But here's the key:
Every line must connect to a real human emotion — not just numbers.

Let me show you how:

1. Final Expenses — Making It Real

I gently ask:

"Have either of you lost someone close recently?"

If they say no:

"Most funerals range from $25,000–$30,000 with medical bills on top. I recommend $50,000 so your family never has to choose between paying bills and burying someone they love."

If they say yes, I follow with:

"Do you remember how much it cost?"

Whatever they tell me becomes our number. Their story sets the baseline—not statistics.

2. Debt — Reminding Them of Reality

I don't just ask about numbers.
I paint the picture:

"You might have a truck, RV, or a boat—but if there's a loan, your family may be upside-down trying to sell it after you're gone."

This isn't fear.
It's clarity.

3. Mortgage — Home vs. Burden

This is where tone matters. I slow down and say softly:

"You've worked hard to build this home. If the worst happens, would you rather leave behind a house full of love... or a mortgage full of stress?"

Silence follows. Then they write the number.

4. Education — Painting the Future

Not all parents want to pay for college, so I observe:

If I see a Texas A&M hat, school photos, or diplomas on the wall, I might smile and say:

"I bet little Emma would make a great Aggie one day."

They laugh. But now we're talking future—not policy.

5. Readjustment Income — The Human Side of Grief

This one matters most.

I often share a real story of a colleague's family:
A father thought he'd be fine without life insurance. His wife unexpectedly passed away. Months later, their daughter began self-harming from grief. He quit his job to care for her. The family went from stable to broken—just like that.

"You might be able to pick up your broken heart and go back to work. But will your spouse? Your kids? How long before life feels normal again?"

That's why I recommend covering income until the youngest child turns 18.

A Story I'll Never Forget – The Client Who Wanted to Wait

Years ago, I met with a man two months from retirement. He said,

"Let's just wait six months—when my pension starts."

I felt it wasn't wise, but I didn't push.
Two months later, his daughter called me, crying.
"My dad passed away last night… We're getting everything together. Can you help us with his policy?"

My heart sank.

I had to tell her… there was no policy. He wanted to wait.

That night, I sat in my truck and cried.
Not because I lost a sale—
But because a family lost time. Lost stability. Lost peace I could have helped provide.

That was the day I promised myself:
I will not let someone delay protection without understanding the cost of waiting.

FIELD NOTE: "People can argue with your opinion.
They can't argue with their own handwriting."

Emotion, Storytelling & Transitioning into Life Insurance (Without Making It Awkward)

Most agents get nervous when it's time to transition into life insurance.

Auto and home feel easy — they're logical, tangible, and visible. You can see a truck. You can point at a roof. But life insurance is different. It's emotional. It's about love, legacy, and the question none of us like to face:

"What happens to my family if I don't come home tomorrow?"
That's why it must flow, not force.
It should feel like a continuation of caring — not a sales pitch.

The Secret? Make It a Human Conversation, Not a Product Pitch

I always tell my team:
"If life insurance feels awkward, it's because you brought it in like a stranger instead of introducing it like family."

It should sound like this:

- "You mentioned your kids earlier — if something unexpected happened, would they be okay financially?"
- "Who depends on your income to keep this home, this life, going?"
- "If tomorrow didn't go as planned, does your family have time to grieve — or would they have to go straight back to work to survive?"

78

Those are not sales questions.
They are love questions.

Why This Works: People Buy Emotion, Not Information

People don't buy life insurance because they understand it.
They buy it because they feel it.

They picture:

- Their spouse trying to pay the mortgage alone.
- Their kids having to move schools.
- A stranger delivering fried chicken at their funeral because no policy was in place.

Insurance is logical on paper... but purchased in the heart.

How I Transition Naturally in Every Appointment

Here's how my review form flows—auto → home → life insurance—like chapters in a story:

1. Auto Insurance – "Let's make sure your vehicles are protected."
2. Home / Property – "Your home is where your story lives — let's safeguard that too."
3. Then, gently...
   "Now let's talk about the one thing that pays for everything we just discussed — your ability to earn income. If that disappeared tomorrow, how would your family manage?"

With that one sentence, the door opens.
Not pushed. Just opened.

Real Story — The Client Who Wanted to Wait Six Months

I'll never forget this one.

There was a client of mine — a good man, close to retirement. We completed his needs analysis and he said:

"Steven, I know we need life insurance. But I retire in six months. Let's just wait until then."

I didn't push. I respected his decision.

Three months later, I got a phone call. Not from him... but from his daughter.

Her voice was trembling.
"Steven... Dad had a heart attack. He's gone. Do we have any coverage?"

I had to tell her the truth:

"No... he wanted to wait."

Silence. Then sobbing.
And I'll be honest — that one hurt.
Because life insurance isn't about closing a sale — it's about protecting a family. And this time, we were too late.

That day changed me.
That's when I stopped "offering" life insurance... and started fighting for families before they ever needed it.

Client-Led Needs Analysis — Let Them Write Their Own Why

One of the most powerful tools in your entire presentation isn't a glossy brochure, a slide deck, or a rehearsed script.

It's a simple sheet of paper.
A pen.
And silence.

Because when the client writes the numbers, they accept the responsibility.
When they calculate the need, they own the solution.

That's why I always remind new agents:

"Never fill out the life insurance needs analysis for the client.
   Hand them the pen — let them write their own number."

Why This Works — Psychology and Ownership

When a client sits across from you with a pen in hand and writes down:

- Their mortgage balance
- Their debt
- Their income
- Their children's names under "future needs"

…everything changes.

It's no longer "your recommendation."
It becomes their decision.

They're no longer being sold to.
They're leading the conversation.

That is ownership.
And ownership leads to action.

How I Set the Stage

I slide the form to them with two pens and say gently:

"Most people don't know how much life insurance they truly need. So instead of me telling you, let's walk through this together. You fill it out — I'll guide you."

Then I pause.
Silence does the work.
Their hand reaches for the pen.

And just like that — the conversation shifts.

The Flow of the Form (Simple, Not Complicated)

I keep the needs analysis form simple — almost like chapters in a story:

Section	What I Say to Guide Them
Final Expenses	"If one of you passed, would you want your family scrambling for funeral costs"… or have it already taken care of?"
Debt	"Vehicles, credit cards, loans - if your income stopped, would your spouse keep up?"
Mortgage / Rent	"This isn't just a house- it's your home. Should it stay in the family no matter what?"
Education	"Do you want your kids to have options? College, trade school, military - or is that up to chance?"
Readjustment Income	"How long would your family need full income to breathe, heal, and figure out what's next a - 1 year, 3 years, until your youngest turns 18?"

Attaching Emotion to Every Number

It's not enough to fill in amounts. The power comes from attaching real stories and real faces to each line.

So I don't say "final expenses."
I say:

"Have you ever lost someone close? Do you remember what the funeral costs were like?"

I don't say "mortgage payoff."
I say:

"This home—these walls, that kitchen table—should it become a blessing your spouse gets to keep... or a burden they're forced to sell?"
Numbers inform.
Emotion moves.

Example: When the Client Sets Their Own Number

I once helped a couple fill out their form. They wrote down:

- $300,000 mortgage
- $40,000 debt
- $50,000 final expenses
- $100,000 for kids' schooling
- 5 years of income replacement at $60,000 a year

They quietly totaled it.

$750,000

The husband looked at me and said, "Steven... I had no idea."
I smiled and said, "That's not my number. That's yours."

I didn't have to "close."
All I said was:

"Would you like me to take care of this for you?"

He whispered, "Yes."

Field Note: "When the client writes the number, your job isn't to convince them anymore — it's to help them protect it."

Objections aren't rejection — they're hesitation. And hesitation doesn't mean they don't want protection. It usually just means they don't understand something yet, or they don't feel ready to make a decision.
Early in my career, I took objections personally. Now I recognize them for what they really are: signs that someone is still engaged in the conversation. Silence is the real enemy. When a prospect objects, it means they're thinking, not gone.

Almost every objection in our business falls into one of three buckets:

- No Need
- No Money
- No Hurry

If you can learn to recognize which one you're hearing — and speak to it with confidence and empathy — closing becomes natural, not forced.

1. No Need — "We're Fine Like We Are."

This objection usually comes from a place of comfort or denial. They believe what they have is "good enough." Your job is not to argue. It's to illuminate.

How to handle it:

- Ask questions instead of pitching.
- Guide them to realize gaps on their own.
- Use their own words from the review form.

Example phrases you might use:
- "You're probably right — you may never need it. But if you did, would your current setup actually protect your family the way you want it to?"
- "I'm not here to sell you more than you need. I'm here to make sure nothing is left uncovered."

People don't change because of pressure — they change because someone helped them see clearly.

2. No Money — "We Just Can't Afford It Right Now."

Most people don't hate insurance — they hate the idea of adding another bill. And in today's world, that's understandable.

How to respond:

- Agree first. Never fight their reality.
- Then reframe it as protection, not a bill.
- Offer smaller solutions instead of giving up.

Example approach:

"I understand. But if it's tight now, imagine how tight it would be if one income disappeared. Let's find something that fits — even if we start small. Something is better than leaving your family with nothing."

This keeps dignity intact. You're not arguing with their budget — you're helping them guard their future.

3. No Hurry — "Let's Think About It" / "We'll Do It Later."

This is the most dangerous objection, because it feels harmless. No anger. No rejection. Just delay. And delay is where most families lose everything.

How to respond wisely:

- Stay calm. Stay respectful.
- Bring them back to the reason they invited you.
- Show finality — not fear, but responsibility.

You might say:

"I get it — this isn't an easy decision. But the only time we can secure coverage is today, while you're healthy and able. The perfect time rarely comes. That's why people call me after a loss and say, 'I wish we had done this sooner.'"

You're not pushing them — you're protecting them from regret.

Field Note: Objections Aren't Walls, They're Windows

"An objection isn't a no. It's simply a request for clarity. Walls end conversations. Windows give you a way through."

Mindset Shift: You're Not Arguing — You're Serving

The way you handle yourself during an objection matters more than the words you use.

Never:

- Roll your eyes.
- Get defensive.
- Debate like a lawyer.

Always:

- Pause. Breathe.
- Let them feel heard.
- Respond with clarity and calm.

Confidence doesn't mean talking louder — it means staying steady when others get unsure.

Transition to the Close

Once you've handled the objection with respect and confidence, don't circle the runway. Land the plane.

A smooth transition might sound like:

"I understand your concern — and that's exactly why these matters. Let's do this: we'll start with a plan that fits your budget today, so at least your family is protected."

Never Ask for Permission to Close

One of the biggest mistakes new — and even experienced — agents make is asking for permission to do their job. They tiptoe around the close like it's something to be ashamed of. They say things like:

"So… do you want to think about it?"
"Would you maybe like to move forward?"
"Do you want to go ahead and do this?"

But here's the truth — when you've listened well, identified their needs, offered real solutions, and shown how it protects their family, you've earned the right to lead the close.

This isn't pressure. This is service backed by confidence.

Why You Don't Ask — You Lead

When you ask timidly, you plant doubt. Your client starts thinking, "If they're unsure… maybe I should be unsure too."

But when you lead, you communicate something entirely different:

"This is important. I believe in it. And I believe in you."

It's not aggressive. It's calm certainty.

Instead of asking permission, you assume the close.
Not in a manipulative way — in a responsible, professional way.

What Confident Closing Sounds Like

You don't ask, "Do you want it?"
You say:

- "Alright, let's get this started so your family is protected today."
- "Let me grab the application — we'll take care of this now."
- "Which option works better for your family — the $250,000 or the $500,000?"

Notice the difference? You're not forcing them. You're guiding them.

Confidence vs. Pressure

Pressure says:
"I need this sale."

Confidence says:
"You deserve this protection."

Clients feel the difference instantly. And whether they admit it or not... people want to be led by someone who is calm, steady, and sure.

A Real Appointment That Changed Everything

Years ago, I was three-quarters through an application before the client even realized we were closing. He stopped, looked up, and said:

"Wait — are we actually doing this today?"

I calmly replied, "Yes, sir. Isn't that what you wanted to do?" He nodded and said, "Yeah... I just thought it would be harder."

From then on, I realized: closing isn't something you ask to do — it's something you guide them into.

Why Agents Struggle to Close

Most agents don't hold back because they don't care.
They hold back because they're afraid of one of three things:

- "What if they get offended?"
- "What if they say no?"
- "What if I come across too pushy?"

But let me ask you this — what's worse?
Being told "no"...
or seeing a family lose everything because no one had the courage to guide them?

Field Note: Courage in Closing

"The close isn't about getting a signature. It's about giving someone the chance to say yes to protecting their tomorrow.

A Simple Closing Flow

Here's a rhythm I follow every time before moving into the close:

1. Summarize their needs in their own words.
   "Earlier you told me if something happened, you want your wife and kids to stay in the house and not struggle. That's what this plan does."
2. Offer two simple options — not five.
   "We can start at $250,000 or $500,000. Which one feels right for your family right now?"
3. Assume the close and begin.
   "Okay, let's get this started for you."
4. Be silent. Let them process.
   Confidence is silent. Insecurity keeps talking.

Congratulate, Don't Keep Selling

The moment a client says "yes" is sacred.

Not because you made a sale — but because they chose to protect the people they love.

This is where many agents make their biggest mistake. They keep talking. They keep selling. They keep explaining features, benefits, riders, cash value — as if the client still has to be convinced.

But the decision has already been made.

When you keep selling after a "yes," you don't build confidence — you create doubt. You make clients question themselves. You risk turning certainty into hesitation.
So instead of selling... you celebrate.

Why This Moment Matters

When a client agrees to protect their family, they're not buying a policy.

They're buying:

- Security.
- Peace of mind.
- A future they can trust.

If you rush past that moment and dive back into charts and numbers, you rob them of the emotional victory they just gave themselves.

Celebrate it with them. Cement that moment in their memory.

What It Sounds Like

Right after they say yes, stop. Look them in the eye, smile, and say something like:

- "Congratulations — this is a smart decision for your family."
- "You just did something today that your future self — and your family — will thank you for."
- "This is leadership. You stepped up to protect the people who matter most."

Then shake their hand or, if appropriate, give a meaningful pat on the shoulder. Let the moment breathe.

The Power of Validation

Selling is about persuasion.
Congratulating is about affirmation.

You're no longer the salesperson at this moment — you're the advisor standing beside them, acknowledging their wisdom and courage.

Clients don't remember the application questions or the policy details years later.
They remember how they felt in that moment.

Real-Life Example

A young couple sat across from me once, exhausted from months of home-buying stress. They were nervous, unsure if they could afford life insurance on top of it.

When they finally said, "Okay... let's do it," I didn't say another word about premiums or policy riders.

I smiled, stood, shook their hands, and said:

"I want you to know — this is one of the best decisions you'll ever make for your family. What you did today is love in action."

The wife teared up. The husband nodded slowly.
From that moment forward, I wasn't their "insurance guy."
I was their trusted person. Their advisor. And to this day — they are still my clients.

Practical Tips for This Moment

- Pause when they say yes. Don't rush.
- Smile and congratulate sincerely — not like a script.
- Don't introduce new products or add-ons right away. There will be time later.
- Let them feel proud, not pressured.
- Finish paperwork gently — no rush, no panic.

Field Note: he Seal of Trust

"The close doesn't end with a signature. It ends with how they feel walking out the door."

Reviews, Referrals, and Reinforcement

Most agents think the close is the end of the appointment.

Top producers know — it's the beginning of the relationship.

You've earned their trust. They've said yes. Their relief is high. Their confidence is fresh. And in that exact moment — before life gets busy again — you have a window to strengthen the bond, plant seeds for referrals, and create long-term loyalty.

Not with pressure.
Not with cheesy lines.
But with gratitude and service.

Why This Moment Is So Powerful

Right after saying yes, clients feel three things at the same time:

> ➤ Relief — "We finally did it."
> ➤ Confidence — "This was the right decision."
> ➤ Trust — "They took care of us."

That emotion fades quickly once daily life returns. That's why you don't wait for "someday" to ask for a review or referral. You plant the seed while the soil is still soft.

How I Transition Naturally

Right after I congratulate them and we finish paperwork, I smile and say something simple like:

"Thank you for trusting me today. If you found this helpful, I'd be grateful if you'd leave a review or share my card with someone you care about. I'm never too busy to take care of the people my clients love."

Then I quietly place three business cards on the table. One for them. Two for people they know.

No pressure. Just an invitation.

Why This Works Without Feeling Pushy

- It's not about you — it's about protecting other families.
- It affirms their decision — not just the policy, but their trust in you.
- It turns clients into advocates, not just customers.

Real-Life Example — The Referral Ripple Effect

I once finished an appointment with a couple who purchased life insurance after weeks of debating it. As they signed, the wife said, "I'm glad we did this."
I congratulated them, then said:

"I appreciate you trusting me. If you ever want me to take care of someone you care about, I'd consider that the highest compliment."

I handed them three cards.

A week later, they sent me their neighbor.
That neighbor referred his brother.
That brother referred a coworker.
Six policies from one single conversation.

Not because I sold hard — but because I served well.

Reinforce the Decision After You Leave

The appointment may be over, but the impression doesn't end there.

Small touches create loyalty that no marketing budget can buy.
Simple follow-ups that go a long way:
- Send a handwritten thank-you card.
- Text when the policy is approved: "Proud of you — your coverage is active."
- Add their first annual review to your calendar before you leave the driveway.
- On holidays or birthdays — send a card before they expect it.

Field Note: Make Trust Last

"Referrals are not given because you asked. They're given because you cared — and they remembered."

Measure, Refine, and Stay Ready

Great closers aren't great by accident. They don't rely on luck, charm, or "good weeks." They build systems. They track their habits. They improve what others ignore.

Most agents guess where their business comes from. Top agents measure it.

Because what gets measured improves. What stays unmeasured eventually disappears.

Why Tracking Matters

The difference between struggle and momentum is usually not talent — it's awareness.

When you track your numbers, you start seeing patterns:
- Where appointments fall apart
- Where clients hesitate
- Where follow-ups are being missed
- Where you are winning consistently

Tracking turns feelings into facts.
And facts are what make you better, faster, and more confident.

The Four Metrics Every Agent Should Track for 90 Days

You don't have to track everything — just the right things.

1. Show-Up Rate
Appointments held ÷ appointments set

- If it's below 70%, you don't have a closing problem —
  you have a confirmation problem.

2. Decision-in-Room Rate
Appointments where a decision was made (yes or no) ÷
appointments held

- Goal: 60%+
- Why? Because chasing people for weeks destroys your
  energy.

3. Celebrate & Ask Rate
Percentage of clients you both congratulated and asked for a
review/referral

- Goal: 80–90%
- This is where future business is born.

4. Referral Cascade
Average number of new policies from each client within 60 days

- If you're not averaging at least 1 referral per 3 new
  clients, you're leaving trust — and income — on the
  table.

How to Track Without Overthinking

You don't need fancy CRM software to start (though it's useful later). A notebook, a spreadsheet, or a whiteboard works fine.

Every day, write down:

- How many people you contacted
- How many appointments you set
- How many showed
- How many decided in the room
- How many you congratulated and asked for a review/referral
- How many referrals came in after

Ten minutes a day. That's it. But the results will change everything.

Refine What You See

Tracking is only the first half.

The second half is sitting down — maybe at the end of each week with a Diet Coke in your truck before heading home — and asking:
- "Where did the conversation feel rushed?"
- "Where did clients get confused?"
- "Did I ask permission or did I guide?"
- "What did I say when they hesitated — and did it work?"
- "What will I do differently this week?"

This is where good agents become great — in quiet reflection before the next call, not during the call.

Stay Ready — Body, Mind, and Spirit

You cannot pour from an empty cup.

If you want to be sharp in every appointment, if you want your mind clear and your presence strong, you can't live burnt out, sleep-deprived, or spiritually dry.

Before I step out of my vehicle for an appointment, I take a breath...
whisper a small prayer...

"Lord, guide my words. Help me serve this family with honesty and courage."

Not for the sale — but for the responsibility.

I believe when your heart is right, your delivery changes. You're not chasing a signature. You're protecting a life.

Field Note: Stewardship Over Sales

"Excellence doesn't start in the presentation. It starts in the preparation — when no one is watching."

Ethics & Trust You Can Sleep With

You can close every deal in this book...
... but if you do it without integrity, none of it matters.

In insurance, your reputation travels faster than your marketing. People may forget your presentation, your rate, even your company name — but they will never forget how you made them feel, especially when things go wrong.

This is more than business. This is stewardship.

Why Ethics Matter More Than Ever

We don't sell gadgets. We don't sell lawnmowers or gym memberships.
We sell promises.

Promises that, one day, someone's spouse will call you — not to start a policy, but to use one. And in that moment, when you hear the shaking voice on the other end of the line... you will either be proud of the policy you placed, or ashamed of the one you pushed.

That's why this chapter exists.

My Rule: If I Wouldn't Sell It to My Own Family... I Don't Sell It at All

It's simple:

- If I wouldn't put my wife and kids on that policy — I won't put yours.
- If a client can get better coverage somewhere else — I tell them.
- If they're overpaying for coverage they don't need — I fix it.

Has it cost me money? Yes.
Has it made me more referrals, trust, and sleep at night?
Absolutely.

Fear is a Tool — Not a Weapon

Insurance deals with real risk — death, storm damage, lawsuits, medical bills.
It's emotional. And yes, fear is part of the conversation.

But there's a difference between:

✓ Illuminating responsibility ("Your family would need time and income to grieve")
✗ Weaponizing fear ("Imagine your wife crying because you didn't care enough...")

One serves. One manipulates.
You can feel the difference in your soul when you say it.

The Weight of a Signature

Every time a client signs a policy, they're really signing something invisible:

They're signing their trust over to you.

That's why you never:

- Hide fees or exclusions in small print
- Underinsure someone just to give them a lower price
- Over insure someone so you can brag on premium volume
- Rush someone into signing without explaining how it works

I've seen agents bind policies knowing they'd never pay out under real loss... just to hit a bonus.

I've also stood at funerals, knowing a widow is okay because of a policy we wrote together. That's the difference between selling and serving.

Story — The Check That Changed Me

Years ago, a young widow came into my office holding a folded check.
Her hands were trembling. Her husband had passed suddenly. We had written his life policy two years prior.

She sat down and whispered, "I don't know what to do now, but because of this... my kids won't lose their home."
She wasn't grateful for the policy.
She was grateful for the time, dignity, and space to grieve that the policy bought her.

That's when I realized — I don't sell insurance.
I sell time. Options. Peace.

And you don't cheapen that with unethical shortcuts.

Ethical Closing Checklist

Ask yourself before every application:

- Would I sell this to my own family?
- Did I explain this so clearly they could explain it back to me?
- If I die tonight, will I still be proud of what I did today?
- If I lose this sale by doing the right thing — am I okay with that?
(If the answer is "no," don't write it.)

Why Clients Stay for Life

People don't stay because you're perfect. They stay because:

- You answer when they call.
- You tell the truth — even when it costs you.

- You fix mistakes instead of hiding them.
- You don't disappear after the policy is signed.

Field Note: Legacy Over Commission

"There are two kinds of agents: those who chase profit, and those who earn trust. Only one of them sleeps well."

Presence, Prayer, and Purpose Before the Appointment

There's a quiet moment before every appointment that nobody sees.

Before I knock on the door, step inside the office, or walk up to the kitchen table... I pause. Sometimes it's in the driver's seat with the engine still running. Sometimes it's standing outside the porch with my bag in hand. And every time, I say a simple prayer:

"Lord, guide my words. Help me serve, not sell. Let me be a blessing in this house."

That moment grounds me.

Not in fear. Not in pressure. But in purpose.

Because if I'm honest, early in my career, I thought closing a sale depended on sounding perfect — having every answer, every rate, every rebuttal memorized. But over time, I learned something bigger:

People don't just want an insurance agent at their table. They want someone who actually cares that they're sitting there.

Prayer reminds me of that.

I'm Not There to Impress Their Wallet — I'm There to Protect Their World

When I pray before I walk in, I'm not asking for a sale. I'm asking for clarity, patience, and the right heart.
I'm asking for:

- The discipline to listen more than I speak.
- The wisdom to tell the truth, even if it costs me the deal.
- The courage to lead the conversation — but the humility to shut up when it's time to listen.
- The strength to accept whatever happens — yes, no, or not yet.

Because appointments go better when I walk in trying to help — not trying to win.

Service Over Sales

You can feel the difference when your purpose is right.

When you walk in thinking "I have to close this," your words get heavy. You overtalk. You rush the process. You start pleading instead of guiding.

But when you walk in thinking, "Lord, let me serve this family well," something shifts.

You speak slower.
You listen deeper.
You notice things — the family pictures on the wall, the tiredness in their voice, the way they look at each other when money gets mentioned.

Prayer doesn't make you religious in the appointment — it makes you present.

Presence Is What Earns Trust

I believe God honors effort. Not perfection — but effort.

So I show up early.
I organize my paperwork.
I rehearse my presentation.
And before I touch the doorknob — I ask for His help.

And you know what I've learned?

People may not hear the prayer — but they always feel the presence that comes from it.

A calm voice.
A steady tone.
A respectful pause before asking hard questions like:

- "Who depends on your income the most?"
- "If tomorrow didn't go as planned… do they stay in this house, or do they lose it?"

That kind of presence doesn't come from memorizing scripts.

It comes from knowing why you're really there.

Field Note: "Before you step into a home, quiet your heart. This job isn't about selling policies — it's about protecting people with honor. Pray, breathe, then knock."

Reviews, Referrals & Reinforcement — Turning a "Yes" Into a Relationship

The moment a client says "Yes," most agents exhale like the job is done.

But top performers understand—that's not the end of the appointment. That's the beginning of the relationship.

Right after the signature is when emotion is at its highest. Relief, pride, peace of mind—this is when clients feel good about the decision they just made. And that's exactly when you reinforce it.

Not by selling more.
Not by piling on extra forms or riders.
But by making them feel appreciated, safe, and confident in their choice.

Step 1: Make Them Feel Proud, Not Pressured

The worst mistake an agent can make after a "yes" is to keep talking.

Don't re-explain the coverage. Don't push endorsements or additional products. Don't talk yourself out of the sale.

Just pause… smile… and say something like:

"Congratulations—you just made a smart decision for your family. They'll never know the stress you just prevented, but you will."

Let them feel it. Let the moment breathe. This is when trust turns into loyalty.

Step 2: Reinforce, Don't Resell

Once they've said yes and you've congratulated them, do three simple things:

- Shake their hand like it matters
- Thank them for trusting you
- Reassure them with confidence, not more sales

I like to say:

"From here forward, this isn't just a policy. You can call me if you need anything—questions, changes, emergencies. You won't have to chase me."

Because people don't stay with you because the premium is lowest.
They stay because they feel taken care of.

Step 3: Ask for Reviews & Referrals—The Right Way

Now that trust is high and emotion is positive, this is the perfect moment to expand your reach—without sounding desperate or salesy.

I keep it simple:

"If I took good care of you today, I'd be honored if you left me a review or shared my card with someone you care about. I'm never too busy to help your family or friends."

Then I hand them three cards.
One for them. Two for the people they care about.
It feels natural—not forced—because it's built on gratitude, not pressure.

Why This Works

- People love to justify good decisions. Asking for reviews or referrals lets them double down on that feeling.
- Referrals come with built-in trust. You don't have to climb the wall—they open the door.
- Reviews live online forever. While you're sleeping, someone is reading it and deciding whether to call you.

Real-Life Example — The Referral Chain

A few years back, I finished an appointment with a young couple who finally decided to protect their family with a life policy. After the paperwork, I congratulated them and said:

"If you ever want your friends or family to feel the same peace you feel right now, here are a few cards. I'll treat them just as well."

They handed one to their neighbor.
That neighbor referred his brother.
His brother sent his coworker.

One appointment became six policies.
Not because I sold hard—because I served well and asked at the right moment.

Final Thought — Chapter 4

Presenting and closing isn't about being the smoothest talker or the smartest person in the room. It's about being present, prepared, and personal.

People don't buy insurance.
They buy security.

They buy confidence in you.
They buy the feeling that when life goes wrong—someone will answer the phone and help put the pieces back together.

A great presentation doesn't just explain coverage.
A great close doesn't just collect a signature.
They both do the same thing — they make a client feel safe enough to say yes.

Because at the end of the day, this business isn't built on products.
It's built on moments like this:

You sat at their table.
You listened.
You cared.
You helped them protect the people they love most.
And when they said "yes," you didn't sell—you congratulated.

Do that consistently—and you won't just close more business... you'll earn a place in people's lives for years to come.

"Excellence is not an act, but a habit."
-   Aristotle

CHAPTER 5: The Freeze Moment

Every agent knows the sentence that steals the air from the room:

"I'm not interested."

The first time you hear it, your chest tightens. Your mouth goes dry. Your brain sprints for the "right line," and all you can feel is the floor tilting under your feet. Early in my career, I treated that phrase like a brick wall. Now I see it for what it really is: a closed door with an unlocked handle.

The freeze moment isn't a verdict. It's a reflex.

Most people aren't rejecting you—they're protecting themselves. They're guarding their time, their budget, and their peace from what they fear might be another pushy sales pitch. And your own body responds in kind—heart rate up, breathing shallow, voice a little tight. That's normal. You're human. The goal isn't to pretend you don't feel it. The goal is to stay steady inside it.

Here's what shifted everything for me:

- I stopped treating objections like fights to win and started treating them like fears to understand.
- I quit racing to talk and learned to breathe, agree, and invite.
- I remembered my job isn't to prove I'm right—it's to make someone feel safe enough to keep talking.

When "I'm not interested" shows up, I give it a little room. One quiet beat. Then, in a calm tone:

"Totally fair—most folks feel the same way at first. My job isn't to sell you something you don't need. I just don't want you exposed to a surprise you didn't see coming. Would a quick look—ten minutes—help us confirm you're in good shape and move on with your day?"

No pressure. No debate. No hard sell. Just an open hand and a low-friction next step.

Because the freeze moment isn't about the perfect script. It's about posture—steady voice, slow pace, shoulders relaxed, eyes kind. When your presence says, "You're safe here," people unfreeze. They consider. They lean in a little.

That's where this chapter begins—not with tricks, but with temperament. If you can stay calm when they tighten up, you've already separated yourself from 90% of agents. You've turned a wall back into a door, and your hand is already on the handle.

Field Note: "In the freeze, don't race for words—reach for calm. Safety opens more doors than cleverness ever will."

What's Happening Under the Hood (To You and To Them)

When an objection hits—"I'm not interested," "We're good where we are," "Not right now"—something happens before a single word comes out of your mouth.

Your body reacts.
Their body reacts.
Two nervous systems reading each other, deciding in seconds whether this moment is safe… or stressful.

Understanding that changes how you handle every objection from here on.

Physiologically — What Happens to You

Even if you don't show it, your body knows.

- Your heart rate jumps.
- Your mouth dries up.
- Your brain scrambles for the "right response."
- Your instinct goes fight, flight, or freeze.

That's not weakness—that's wiring. You're not trying to eliminate that feeling. You're learning how to ride it without letting it steer the wheel.

That's why techniques like the 5-Second Reset work. They aren't sales tactics—they're control tactics. They give your nervous system 5 seconds to let the fear pass through you instead of taking over.

Psychologically — What's Happening to Them

Most objections aren't personal.

They're not saying:

- "I don't like you."
- "You're bad at this."
- "Insurance is worthless."

They're really saying:

- "I don't want to make a mistake."
- "Are you going to pressure me?"
- "Is this conversation going to cost me time, money, or comfort?"

In other words—they aren't rejecting your solution, they're rejecting the stress they assume comes with it.

They aren't fighting you.
They're protecting themselves.

The Reframe That Changed Everything

Once you understand this, you stop arguing with their words... and start addressing their worry.

The freeze moment isn't a stop sign.
It's an alarm.

Your job isn't to break the door down.
It's to lower the volume... and invite them to open it.

Practical Shift You Can Use Today

Instead of reacting with:

- "But just hear me out."
- "You don't even know what I'm offering yet."
- Getting flustered, speeding up, sounding desperate...

Respond with:

- Calm.
- Agreement.
- An invitation—not a push.

Example:

"I completely understand. Most people feel the same at first. My job isn't to sell you something you don't need—just to make sure you're not missing something important. Would you be open to a quick look?"

Field Note: "Objections aren't personal. They're protective. The moment you understand that—you stop resisting the objection and start guiding the person."

The 5-Second Reset — Staying Steady When Your Mind Wants to Sprint

When someone pushes back—"Not interested," "We're fine," "Maybe later"—most agents react too fast.

They rush to answer.
They talk faster.
They try to fill the silence.

And in doing so—they lose trust.

What separates top producers isn't that they never feel panic—it's that they never let panic speak first.

That's where the 5-Second Reset becomes a game changer.

Why You Need It

In the freeze moment, your body fires before your brain does.

- Heart rate jumps
- Thoughts race
- You feel the urge to do something—anything—quickly

The reset is your anchor. It gives your voice time to catch up to your values.

Because the first words after an objection decide everything—
whether the door stays cracked open or slams shut.

The Reset (Simple. Calm. Real.)

Here's how it works in real conversations—not as a cheesy script, but as a rhythm:

1. Pause (1 second)
Let the objection land. Don't rush. Silence is not your enemy—it's your ally.

2. Agree (1 sentence)

"I completely understand—most people feel the same way at first."

Agreement relaxes defenses. It tells their brain, "This isn't a fight."

3. Disarm (1 sentence)

"I'm not here to sell you something you don't need."

This lowers pressure and shows respect.

4. Reframe (1 sentence)

"I just want to make sure you're not exposed to something avoidable."

Now it's not about you selling—it's about them staying protected.

5. Invite (1 sentence)

"Would you be open to a quick 10-minute look, just to confirm you're covered?"

That's it.
No pressure.

No debate.
Just calm leadership.

Why This Works — Scientifically and Emotionally

- The pause calms your nervous system.
- The agreement calms theirs.
- The disarm removes fear.
- The reframe adds purpose.
- The invitation gives direction.

Objections aren't battles to win. They're moments to breathe, agree, and lead.

Real Talk — What This Sounds Like in My Office

Early in my career, I used to jump in with rehearsed rebuttals. Fast. Defensive. Sounded desperate.

Today? It's slower. Softer. More confident.

I've said this exact line hundreds of times:

"Totally fair—I respect that. Most folks feel the same way at first. I'm not here to pressure you—just to make sure you're not missing something that could cost you down the road. Would 10 minutes be fair?"

Not once has someone gotten angry at that.
Some say yes.
Some say no.
But all of them stay calm—and that's the win.

Field Note: "You don't have to rush to win. Calm is stronger than cleverness in every objection."

Feel, Found, Felt — The Quiet Power of Empathy in Objections

Some agents hear an objection and go straight into defense mode.

They explain harder.
They talk faster.
They push.

But when someone hesitates, they don't need more information—they need to feel understood.

That's why one of the most timeless objection tools I use (and still teach to my team) is the Feel, Found, Felt Method.

It's gentle.
It's human.
And it works—because it lets people keep their dignity while you guide them forward.

The Flow (Simple but Powerful)

1. FEEL — Acknowledge their concern, without resistance.

"I completely understand how you feel."

This tells them:
You're safe. I'm listening. You're not wrong for asking that.

2. FOUND — Show they're not alone. Others felt the same.

"A lot of families I work with have found themselves feeling the exact same way…"

This removes shame. It normalizes their hesitation.

3. FELT — Show where others landed after gaining clarity.

"…but once they saw how this protected their family, they felt confident moving forward."

This paints a path from hesitation → peace.

Real Life Example — The Hesitant Couple

A few years back, I sat at a young couple's dining table. Kids' toys were scattered across the floor, dinner dishes still in the sink. They needed life insurance—badly—but they were overwhelmed.

Halfway through the presentation, the husband leaned back and said:
"Steven, I just don't know if it's the right time. Maybe when things settle down financially."

I didn't argue. I didn't rush.
I took a breath and said:

"I completely understand how you feel. Most young families I meet feel the same way—there's always something that seems more urgent. But after we walk through what this actually does for your kids when life doesn't go as planned... they feel relieved that they did it now rather than later."

He looked at his wife.
She nodded.
We finished the needs analysis together and found an amount that fit their budget.

They said yes—not because I pushed… but because they felt safe.

Why This Works

- It meets emotion with empathy, not education
- It keeps the conversation collaborative, not confrontational
- It shifts the client's imagination—from "risk of buying" to "risk of not acting"
- It protects their dignity—no arguing, no ego, no pressure

Practical Tips to Use This Naturally

- Don't rush the lines—slow is powerful.
- Use their language back to them ("right time," "tight budget," "nervous to commit").
- Pair with soft body language—open posture, calm voice, eye contact.
- Always pause after each part—let the words land.
- Personalize the "felt" step with something true—not a cliché.

Field Note:

"People don't follow the agent with the best script. They follow the one who makes them feel understood."

Pattern Interrupts — Turning "Not Interested" into an Open Door

Every objection has a rhythm.
You've heard it a hundred times:

"I'm not interested."
"We're fine with what we have."
"We'll think about it."

Those words can shut most agents down. But top producers?
They don't argue. They don't push harder. They simply interrupt the pattern.

A pattern interrupt is not about being clever.
It's about being calm, respectful, and unexpected—just enough to break their automatic wall and open a real conversation.

Why Pattern Interrupts Work

When a prospect hears "insurance," their brain goes on autopilot defense mode. They assume:

- You're going to pressure them.
- This will waste their time.
- They need to shut this down fast.

So they respond with automatic protection phrases—not because they don't need you, but because they don't trust the process.

A good pattern interrupt does three things in seconds:

1. Acknowledges their resistance without fighting it.
2. Creates curiosity.
3. Redirects the energy gently back to value.

Simple Phrases That Break the Pattern (Respectfully)

Here are real lines I use in the field and teach to my team:

- "Totally fair. Most people felt the same way before they saw this one thing that surprised them. Mind if I show you? 90 seconds—no pressure."
- "I hear you. Quick question—if there was a blind spot in your coverage, would you want to at least know about it?"
- "No problem at all. Just so I don't bother you again—are you all set on liability limits and income protection, or should we cross it off together?"
- "Absolutely understand. Out of curiosity, if your current agent retired tomorrow, who would you call first?"

Each line does the same thing:
Acknowledges. Calms. Redirects. Invites.

Real-Life Story — The Warehouse Manager

A year ago, I walked into a distribution warehouse. The office was buzzing, forklifts beeping, papers everywhere. I introduced myself to the operations manager—he didn't even sit down.

He crossed his arms and said, "Not interested."

Old me might've panicked. But I took a breath and quietly said:

"Totally fair. Most managers tell me the exact same thing— especially if everything is running smooth.

Two quick things, and I'll get out of your way.
• I'm not here to sell you anything today.

• I just noticed a lot of warehouses are underinsured on business interruption—if a supplier delay hits, payroll stops in 30 days. Are you covered for that?"

He paused. Uncrossed his arms.
"Email me something," he said.

Two days later, that turned into a full review.
That review turned into policies.
Those policies turned into a referral to their CPA.

All from one calm, respectful interruption.

How to Deliver Pattern Interrupts Naturally

- Posture: Relaxed shoulders. Calm eye contact. No leaning forward aggressively.
- Tone: Slow. Steady. Curious—not salesy.
- Timing: Use after the objection, not over it. Let them finish.
- Intent: Not to "win." But to keep the door cracked open.

Field Note: "You're not fighting objections—you're freeing people from their own reflexes."

Framing Their Fear — Handling "Let Me Think About It"

When a client says, "Let me think about it," most new agents hear no.

It's not a no.
It's fear.

Not fear of you... but fear of making the wrong choice. Fear of committing to something they don't fully understand. Fear of being pressured. Fear of buying—then regretting it.

If you treat "let me think about it" like a wall, you back away, pack your bag, and leave the kitchen table defeated. But if you treat it for what it really is—hesitation wrapped in uncertainty—you'll realize something powerful:

They don't want to say no.
They just don't feel safe enough to say yes.

And that is your opportunity—not to push harder—but to lead gently.

Why "I Need to Think About It" Isn't the Real Issue

Behind those five words are unspoken thoughts like:

- "What if I make a bad decision?"
- "What if this is just a sales pitch?"
- "Is this really as important as they say?"
- "Can I trust them?"

They are not rejecting the product.
They're protecting themselves from a mistake.

Your job is not to argue.
Your job is to lower the fear and raise the clarity.

How I Respond — Calm, Steady, No Pressure

I learned this from my old manager, Mark, during one of his mock-review trainings.

When someone tells me, "We just want to think about it," I smile and say:

"I think that's a great idea. This is important, and it deserves thought. Here's something most people don't know— it normally takes 30 to 60 days for a life insurance company to fully approve a policy.

That's their way of saying, 'Let us think about you.'

There's no obligation during that time. Until the policy is approved and you sign off, you're in full control.

So while the company thinks about you... why don't we go ahead and get the application started while you think about it too?"

Silence.
Then a nod.
Then the pen slides across the table.

That's not pressure.
That's leadership.

Why This Works

- It respects their hesitation, instead of fighting it.
- It keeps momentum instead of letting the conversation die.
- It moves them from theory to action—without forcing them to decide today.
- It gives them time, but keeps you in the story.

Most people don't actually go home and think about it. Life gets busy. Kids need homework help. Dinner needs cooking. Your form gets buried under three bills and a pizza coupon.

But when they've already signed the application, thinking becomes real, not abstract.

Real-World Example

I once sat with a young couple on a tight budget. They agreed they needed coverage… but as I finished the proposal, the husband leaned back and said the familiar words:

"We just need to think about it."

Years earlier, I would've stood up and left quietly.
But instead, I said:

"I understand. Most great decisions deserve some thought. The insurance company is going to take 30–60 days to think about you anyway. During that process, you're not locked in—you can cancel, change, or walk away.

So while they think about you… let's go ahead and submit the application—so you still get to think about it too, without risking being unprotected."

They looked at each other. Then nodded.

Thirty-eight days later, the policy was approved. When I called to let them know everything was good to go, the husband said quietly:

"Let's issue it."

No more hesitation. No second appointment. Just peace of mind.

Practical Ways to Handle This Objection

- Use empathy first.
"Totally understand—this is a big decision."

- Name what they're really afraid of.
"Sounds like you just want to make sure this is the right fit. That makes sense."

- Offer shared perspective.
"A lot of families I work with felt the same way at first."

- Reframe the timeline.
"It takes 30–60 days for underwriting. During that time—you can still think, adjust, or cancel."

- Lead confidently to the next step.
"Let's go ahead and get this part started while you take the time you need."

Field Note: People don't freeze because they don't care. They freeze because they care deeply— and don't want to make the wrong move.

Confidence vs. Pressure

There's a fine line between confidently leading a client… and pressuring them.

One earns trust.
The other breaks it.

Clients can't always explain the difference, but they can feel it.

Confidence says, "I know this will help you — let me guide you."
Pressure says, "I need this sale — please don't say no."

One makes people lean in.
The other makes them pull away.

The Real Difference

Confidence	Pressure
Calm, steady tone	Fast talking and nervous energy
Guided leadership	Chasing and convincing
Focused on value to the client	Focused on making a sale
Comfortable with silence	Fills every second with words
Detached from outcome	Desperate to win the outcome
Leaves people feeling safe	Leaves people feeling cornered

I tell my agents all the time:

"You are not here to push. You are here to protect.
And protection requires confidence — not desperation."

How Clients Feel the Difference (Even If They Don't Say It)

Clients won't tell you, "You're being too pushy." They'll just say:

- "Let us think about it."
- "Leave your card."
- "We'll call you next week."
- Or worse, they just disappear.

Not because they don't need insurance...

But because something in your tone told them, "This is about the agent — not about me."

A Real-Life Story — The Quiet Close

I sat across from a couple who clearly needed life insurance.
They weren't rejecting me; they were unsure and afraid of being pressured.

I could see it—the crossed arms, the leaning back, the guarded faces.

Years ago, I would've talked faster. I would've tried harder to convince.
But this time, I leaned back too and simply said:

"This is a big decision. I'm not here to pressure you.
My job is to guide you, whether you move forward tonight or not.
I just want you to know what your options are — clearly and honestly."

The husband uncrossed his arms. The tension broke.

Ten minutes later, they said, "Let's do it."

Not because I pushed… but because I didn't.

How to Project Confidence (Not Pressure)

- Slow Down Your Words
Fast talk = nervous energy. Calm pace = control.

- Use Silence — Don't Fear It
Let your words land. Let them think. Silence builds trust.

- Stand/Sit with Purpose
Feet grounded. Hands visible. Shoulders relaxed. The body
speaks before the mouth does.

- Believe in the Value
You're not selling a policy — you're protecting a family.
Confidence comes when you believe that deep down.

- Detach from the Outcome
Say to yourself: "If they say no, I'm still okay. My job is to serve,
not to sell."
Clients feel that.

Field Note: Pressure says, "I need you." Confidence says, "I'm
here for you." One chases. The other leads.

Soft Language That Leads — Not Pushes

Instead of saying:
- "You need to sign today."
Try:
- "Let's get this started so your family is protected tonight."

Instead of:
- "What do you want to do?"
Try:
- "Here are the two best options — which one feels like a better fit for your family?"

Instead of:
- "Do you want to buy it?"
Try:
- "Let's make sure this is taken care of the right way."

Why This Matters

If people feel pressured, they run.
If people feel heard, they follow.

Pressure sells a policy.
Confidence builds a relationship.

And in this business — relationships are everything.

Real Life Story — The Lost Sale That Taught Me Everything

Early in my career, I lost a sale that should've been a life-changing account—commercial policies, vehicles, buildings, the whole deal. I walked into that meeting hungry. Too hungry. I didn't see a family or a business. I saw commission. I saw numbers. I saw my name on the leaderboard.

The owner was polite but firm.
"I've been with my agent for years. I'm not looking to switch."

And instead of honoring that loyalty, I panicked.

I talked too fast.
I kept pushing.
I tried to convince him instead of serve him.

Within minutes, I could feel the door shutting. He stood up, shook my hand, and said, "I respect your effort, but we're not interested."

I walked out sick to my stomach. Not because I lost the money—because I knew I didn't show up as the kind of agent I promised myself I'd be.

The Lesson I'll Never Forget

For weeks, I replayed that moment.

- If I had slowed down...
- If I had respected his loyalty...
- If I had positioned myself as a backup—not a replacement...
- If I had simply said, "I understand. Let me be a second set of eyes whenever you need me."

…he might not have bought that day, but he would've trusted me tomorrow.

And here's the crazy part—

About a year later, my phone rang.

Same business owner.
His agent had dropped the ball on a claim.
He said, "Can we talk?"

This time I didn't push. I listened. I served. I earned his trust—and the account.

Not because I chased it… but because I waited with integrity.

What Changed?

That loss taught me something no sales book ever could:

Objections aren't barriers — they're mirrors.
They don't show you who the client is.
They show you who you are in that moment.

Was I desperate? Or was I dependable?
Was I trying to sell? Or was I trying to serve?

The client didn't reject insurance. He rejected pressure.
And later—he didn't choose me because of what I said.
He chose me because I was still there, steady, professional, and willing to help without ego.

Field Note:

Clients will forget your pitch, your rate, even your company name…

but they will never forget how you made them feel when they said "no."

How to Apply This Right Now

- Never fight loyalty — honor it.
"Staying with someone who's taken care of you is admirable. If you ever need a second opinion, I'm here."

- Detach from the outcome — stay steady.
People follow calm confidence, not panic.

- Stay in their story, even if they tell you no.
A kind follow-up message.
A Christmas card.
A phone call after a storm.
That's how doors reopen.

- Let your reputation speak louder than your pitch.
Pressure fades. Service lasts.

The Objection Toolkit — Your Calm in the Storm

When a prospect pushes back, it's easy to get flustered—start talking faster, defending your point, or trying to "win" the moment. But objections aren't battles to win. They're chances to guide.
That's why you need a simple framework. Not a script. A rhythm. Something you can rely on when your heart rate jumps and the room gets quiet.

This is the Objection Toolkit I use every day. It keeps me grounded. It keeps the client respected. And it keeps the door open—no matter how the conversation ends.

The 5-Part Objection Toolkit

Step	What It Means	Example
1. Listen Fully	Don't interrupt. Let them finish their thought completely. That's where the real objection lives.	" I get it - go ahead."
2. Validate	Show respect. Validate their concern without agreeing or arguing.	"I completely understand why you feel that way."
3. Reframe	Shift the angle. Turn the objection into a shared concern you can solve together.	"Most families I work with felt the same way until they realized…"
4. Lead with Value	Bring clarity - not pressure. Educate, don't overpower.	"Let me show you one quick thing that surprised them."
5. Offer the Next Step	Don't leave them hanging. Always end with a clear, simple path forward.	

Examples of Soft, Strong Language That Works

Instead of pushing—guide.

- "I completely understand. Most people feel the same way before they see what the risk actually looks like."
- "Just so I don't waste your time—would it help if we double-check this together?"
- "If everything's perfect, I'll be the first to celebrate it with you."
- "I'm not here to sell you something—you may not even need me. But if there's a gap, I'd rather you hear it now instead of after something happens."

These aren't lines. They're postures.

Your Number One Job in an Objection

People don't need more pressure. They need more certainty.
Not louder words. Clearer words.

- You do that by staying calm.
- Speaking slow.
- Asking questions, not delivering speeches.
- And leading them toward a choice—not into a corner.

Avoid These Common Mistakes

- Talking faster to "outsmart" the objection
- Debating or arguing ("But your agent..." "But my rate...")
- Over-explaining until the client feels overwhelmed
- Leaving without offering a next step
- Taking it personal

Real-Life Reminder

Objections are rarely about you.
They're about fear, uncertainty, timing, pride, or past experiences.
Your role isn't to overpower their fear. It's to stand calmly beside it and say:

"Let's look at this together—no pressure, just clarity."

When you take that approach, the objection becomes a bridge—not a wall.

Field Note:
Confidence listens.
Pressure argues.
The one who stays calm—wins trust.

Common Objections & How to Pivot Them

Every agent hears the same objections over and over. The words may change slightly, but the fear behind them is usually the same.

This section is not about memorizing scripts. It's about understanding why people say what they say — and knowing how to calmly guide the conversation forward without pressure.

- Objection #1: "I'm not interested."

What they really mean:
"I don't see the value yet," or "I don't want to be sold."

How to pivot (soft, confident, no pressure):

"I completely get that — most people feel the same way before they know what they're actually protected from.
Would it be okay if I take 60 seconds just to show you one thing most people are surprised they don't have covered? If it's not useful, I'll leave you alone."

Why it works:
You honor their guard without pushing. You offer value, not a sales pitch. You ask permission — which lowers defenses.

- Objection #2: "I already have an agent."

What they really mean:
"I'm loyal," or "I don't want conflict."

How to pivot:

"That loyalty says a lot about you — I respect that. I'm not here to replace anyone. I'd just like to be a second set of eyes. If everything's perfect, I'll be the first to tell you so."

Follow-up question:

"When was the last time your current agent sat down with you and walked through your coverages line by line?"

Why it works:
You're not attacking their agent. You're offering reinforcement. Professional, not predatory.

- Objection #3: "I don't have time."

What they really mean:
"This might waste my time," or "I'm busy and overwhelmed."

How to pivot:
"I completely understand — most business owners I talk with feel the same way. That's why I keep it short and focused. Would 10 minutes early next week be easier — Monday or Thursday?"

Alternate (in-person):
"No problem — just so I don't bother you again, is everything 100% up-to-date with your liability, business interruption, and replacement cost numbers? If so, I'll get out of your way."

Why it works:
You respect their time and give a clear path forward instead of pleading for a meeting.

- Objection #4: "Let me think about it."

What they really mean:
"I'm unsure," "I'm scared to make a bad decision," or "I don't want to be rushed."

How to pivot (your real rhythm — the underwriting approach):

"I think that's fair. This is an important decision. Just so you know, it usually takes 30 to 60 days for the insurance company to review and approve an application — that's their way of saying, 'Let us think about you.'

During that time, you're not locked in. You can change your mind at any point until you approve it.

So while they think about you, why don't we go ahead and get the application started while you think about it too?"

Why it works:
It removes pressure, keeps momentum, and gives them time — without losing the process.

Field Note: Objections aren't rejection. They are a request for safety, clarity, or time. Give them that — without losing your leadership.

The Silent Close — Why the First to Speak Loses

There comes a moment in every presentation when the numbers are on the table.

You've listened. You've built trust.
You've connected their fears and goals to a real solution.
You've presented the coverage and the price.

And now—it's quiet.

Most new agents panic in that silence. They start discounting, explaining more, or filling the air with nervous words like:

- "But wait, that also includes…"
- "It's really a good deal because…"
- "If you want, I can try to get it cheaper…"

That's the worst thing you can do.

Because in that quiet moment—the client isn't rejecting you.
They're deciding.
They're running the numbers in their head.
They're imagining the protection in place—or imagining the regret if they walk away.

If you interrupt that moment—the spell breaks.
You pull them out of their own thoughts and back into defense.

So here's the rule:
After you present the price—stop talking. The first person to
speak loses.

Not because this is a game.
Not because the goal is to "win."

It's because the silence is not your enemy—it's your ally.

In that silence, they are selling themselves.
They're thinking about their kids. Their home. Their business.
Their future.

Let them.

Here's exactly how it looks in real life:

You finish your proposal, slide the paper forward, and say:

144

"For everything we talked about—your home, both vehicles, liability coverage, and life insurance to protect your family— we're at $247 per month.

I'd be honored to put this in place for you."

Then you stop.

No more words.
No nervous laugh.
No "but if it's too much I can go lower."

You stay calm. Confident. Silent.

Because pressure talks. Leadership listens.

Why This Works

- Silence creates space for ownership.
People don't buy because you kept talking. They buy because it became real in their mind.

- Silence shows confidence—not desperation.
If you can sit quietly, it tells them you believe in the value. You're not begging for a yes.

- Silence brings objections to the surface.
If they have a concern, they'll voice it. That gives you something real to address. You can't solve what stays hidden.

Field Note: "After you present the price—say nothing. The silence isn't empty. It's the sound of them deciding if they trust you."

FINAL THOUGHT

The Art of Turning "No" Into "Not Yet"

Every great agent has a moment they'll never forget — not the first "yes," but the first "no" that cut deep. The one that made them question if they were even meant for this business. I've been there too. But if this chapter has taught you anything, I hope it's this:

Objections aren't endings. They're invitations.
Not invitations to argue or push — but to guide, understand, and
　　lead.

Most people don't reject insurance. They reject pressure. They reject confusion. They reject the fear of making a wrong decision. They're not saying, "Go away," as much as they're whispering, "Can I trust you?"

And in that moment — how you respond defines who you are in this business.

- If you get defensive, the door closes.
- If you panic, you lose control.
- But if you breathe, steady yourself, and lead with
　confidence instead of pressure…
　the door often opens just a little wider.

Because people don't follow the loudest voice — they follow the calmest one.

What We're Really Doing Here

We're not just overcoming objections.
We are:

- Lowering fear, not winning arguments

146

- Protecting families, not chasing commissions
- Turning hesitation into understanding
- Transforming "no" into "not yet" — and eventually into "thank you"

Objections stop feeling like rejection once you understand this: Most people want to say yes — they just need someone to make it feel safe to do so.

Field Note: "A 'no' handled with grace often becomes a "yes" handled with trust."

Your Call to Action

As you walk into your next appointment, remember:

- Pause before you respond.
- Lead with empathy, not ego.
- Use the tools — 5 Second Reset, Feel–Found–Felt, Pattern Interrupts — not as scripts, but as anchors.
- And above all… stay human.

Because in the end, people don't remember the presentation.
They remember the person who stayed calm when they felt unsure —
The one who listened, cared, and didn't give up at the first sign of resistance.

This is the art of turning "no" into "yes."
Not by force. Not by tricks.
But by quiet leadership — the kind that earns trust, honors people, and builds a career that lasts.

" To serve is to lead. "
- *Og Mandino*

CHAPTER 6: Building Long -Term Clients

Legacy isn't built by sales. It's built by the people who stay.

In the world of insurance, anyone can sell a policy. But not everyone can keep a client.

Sales can make you money.
Retention builds your agency.
Loyalty builds your legacy.

You can write 50 policies this month, post the numbers on Facebook, hit a leaderboard, and feel like you're on top of the world... but if half of those clients leave by renewal time, you're just running on a hamster wheel — always moving, going nowhere.
The agents who win in the long run aren't the ones who close one big month.
They're the ones whose clients stay year after year...
...and send their kids, their neighbors, and their pastor to you.

From Policies to People

Every policy is a promise.
Not a transaction. Not a quota. A promise.

A promise that says:
"When life goes wrong — when storms hit, when someone dies, when someone gets sued or loses everything — I'll help you put the pieces back together."

That's why building long-term clients requires a mindset shift:

✗ Transactional thinking says: "Sale complete."
☑ Relational thinking says: "Our relationship just started."

When I first began in this business, I chased sales like most agents. I loved the thrill of a signature and the commission that followed. But after a year, I noticed something painful — I was losing as many clients as I was gaining. I wasn't building a business. I was plugging holes in a sinking boat.

Then it clicked:

If they don't stay, you don't grow.
If they don't trust you, they won't refer you.
If they don't feel cared for, they'll find someone who does.

That realization changed my entire approach.

Why Retention Is Everything

Retention isn't flashy. You don't get trophies for it. Leadership rarely sends emails saying: "Congratulations — 93% of your clients stayed!"

But retention is what puts food on the table every month — not just once, but every month for years… for decades.

Think about this:

Metric	Transactional Agent	Relational Agent
New Policies	50	25
Clients Lost	30	03
Net Growth	20	22
Years From Now	Burned out	Book of business paying them every morning

One agent chases policies every month.

The other wakes up to automatic renewals.

A Book of Business Is a Forest — Not a Field

I like to think of clients like seeds.

A seed might sprout quickly...
...but without water, sunlight, and care — it dies just as fast.

But when a seed is nurtured, it grows roots. It grows branches. It provides shade, shelter, and fruit for years to come.

Clients are the same.
You can spend your whole career planting seeds you'll never see again...
Or you can build a forest that feeds your family, your team, and one day — your children.

That forest isn't built by selling.
It's built by staying.

Real Life Example — The Power of Staying in Touch

One of my longest-standing clients started with a simple home and auto policy.

I didn't move on. I stayed in touch.

- I called every renewal.
- I stopped by during storm season to check on their roof.
- I remembered birthdays.
- I asked about their kids by name.

Over time, that one policy became:

- Three generations of auto policies
- A business policy
- Life insurance on both parents
- Referrals to neighbors, cousins, and in-laws

That never would've happened if I treated them like a line on a spreadsheet.

Shifting from Transactional to Relational

Most agents stop serving the moment they stop selling. The policy is written, the commission hits, and they move on to the next lead.

But top producers know that the signature isn't the finish line — it's the starting gun.

Every time a client chooses you, they're not just buying a policy. They're trusting you with their home, business, finances, and family. That trust is sacred.

Why Clients Stay — or Leave

Clients don't leave over price as often as people think.
They leave because:

- They feel unseen.
- Their agent only calls when payment declines.
- They feel like a number, not a name.
- Their questions go unanswered.
- Their rate increased — and no one explained why.

On the flip side, clients stay when:
- You show up before they call.

- You're honest — even when it's uncomfortable.
- You serve, not sell.
- You make them feel like you're in this with them.

One of the best ways I've retained clients is by being honest when things go wrong — especially during rate increases.

When Rates Rise — Tell the Truth

Some agents try to defend the carrier.
Others go silent and hope the client won't notice.

That approach loses clients.

When rates increase, I take a different route. I call my clients personally when I can and say:

"I get it — I'm feeling it too. My rates went up too, and as a father with a family and bills, I know this puts a strain on people. But here's what I can do — let's walk through some options together."

No excuses. No corporate talk. Just honesty and solutions.

Result?
People may not love the rate — but they trust me. And when trust stays, so do they.

Mastering the Art of Check-Ins

Check-ins aren't sales calls — they're relationship builders.

They take five minutes, but they pay for years.

Simple ways to check-in:

- "Just wanted to make sure everything's still fitting your needs."
- "Storm's coming this week — y'all doing okay? Anything you need?"
- Handwritten birthday card
- Quick text on renewal month: "Want me to review anything before it renews?"

People don't leave agents they feel connected to.
They leave when silence settles in.

Real Life Story: Serving Through Loss

Years ago, one of my clients was killed in a tragic car accident caused by an uninsured motorist. Her 18-year-old daughter called me — heartbroken, overwhelmed, and lost.

She didn't know what to do.
She didn't know how to file a claim.
She didn't have life insurance on her mom.
She didn't even know how they were going to pay for the funeral.

So I stepped in.

- I filed the uninsured motorist claim for her.
- I talked directly with the adjusters.
- I found where her mom's policy had medical and funeral benefit coverage.
- I made sure the check was processed quickly so they could bury her with dignity.

She later told me, "You weren't just her insurance agent — you were our lifeline."

That's why this business matters. That's why you don't quit on people after they sign.

Leveraging Renewals as Growth Opportunities

Most agents see renewals as routine — something automatic.
Top agents see them as the best opportunity to grow deeper roots.

When a renewal approaches, you're not just checking coverage.
You're checking in on a relationship.

Life doesn't stand still between renewals. Kids graduate.
Homes are bought. Businesses expand. People change jobs,
retire, or lose loved ones.

A renewal is your chance to stop and ask:

"What's new in your life since last year?"

That one question has built more trust for me than any sales pitch
ever could.

Why Renewals Matter

Every renewal represents trust already earned.
You're not cold-calling. You're not convincing. You're
reconnecting.

When handled with care, a renewal can:
- Uncover new coverage needs
- Strengthen loyalty
- Lead to new referrals
- Prevent cancellations before they happen

It's the difference between chasing growth and compounding
growth.

The Second Sale Philosophy

If the first sale is trust, the second is loyalty.

Once someone says "yes" to you, they've already crossed the hardest bridge — belief.
The second sale, whether it's a homeowner's policy, life policy, or business coverage, isn't about convincing anymore. It's about serving the next chapter of their life.

When a client trusts me with their auto insurance, I see it as the start of a relationship.
So later, I'll say:

"Now that we've got your auto squared away, let's look at your home. I'd like to make sure everything you've worked hard for is protected under one plan that fits your goals."

It's not upselling — it's up-serving.

Over time, that one client becomes a multi-policy household:
Auto → Home → Life → Small business → Children's policies → Retirement coverage.

Each sale grows easier, because each sale deepens the relationship.

And eventually, those clients begin referring friends — because they don't just trust my product; they trust me.

Real Life Example — One Renewal That Changed Everything

I once had a young couple who started with a basic auto policy. They were newly married, living in a small rental house, and just starting out. When renewal came, I gave them a call and simply asked, "What's new this year?"

They laughed and said, "Actually, we just bought a house — and we've got a baby on the way."

That conversation turned into a homeowners policy and life insurance for both parents. Their premium went up, but so did their peace of mind.

A few months later, the husband's brother called. Then their neighbor. Then a coworker.

That one renewal call grew into twelve households, three business accounts, and years of steady referrals.

That's the power of staying connected.

Turning Clients into Referral Engines

Happy clients are good.
Referring clients are gold.

Referrals aren't luck — they're earned through consistent care.

At the end of every appointment, I'll simply say:

"If I've done a good job for you today, would you be willing to help me help someone you care about?"

Then I hand them three business cards.
No pressure. No pitch. Just a simple request.

It works because it's authentic. It comes from gratitude, not greed.
And it keeps me top of mind when someone they love needs help.

Real Life Example – The Patron Saint of Savings

Years ago, back when I was a captive agent, I started getting calls from Catholic priests across South Texas.
It all began when a new priest from Poland needed car insurance.
The rectory didn't know what to do — he had no U.S. history, no credit, and no English. My dad gave them my number.

After a few long calls with underwriting and some prayer, I got it done.

From then on, the priests started calling me one by one.
Each time, I helped them as best I could — and before I knew it, my colleagues had a running joke in the office.
They said, "Here comes Steven, the Patron Saint of Savings!"

I didn't mind it.
I wore that nickname with pride — because it meant I was helping people who truly needed it. And those priests became lifelong clients and some of my biggest advocates.

They weren't high-commission policies.
But they were high-trust relationships.
And trust pays forever.

The Crawfish Tradition — How Community Builds Loyalty

Back in my captive days, my friend and fellow agent Donny had an idea: A crawfish boil for clients.

At first, it was just a few tables in his backyard — a couple of folding chairs, some music, and good food. But word spread fast. Within a few years, it grew into one of the biggest community events in town.

We had snow cones for kids, music playing, raffle prizes, and laughter that could be heard for blocks. Clients didn't just show up — they stayed. They mingled. They connected.

At its peak, more than 250 people came.
Families, small business owners, retirees, new homeowners — everyone showed up because they felt like part of something.

It wasn't business anymore.
It was belonging.

That's when I learned one of the most powerful truths in sales:
"People may buy from you once because of a quote.
They stay with you for years because of connection."

Bringing the Tradition Forward

Now that I have my independent agency, I plan to bring that tradition back.
Maybe it won't be crawfish.
Maybe it'll be barbecue, brisket, or just a warm meal on a cool Texas evening.

But the heart of it will be the same — food, laughter, and fellowship.
A day where clients and community come together, not for business, but for gratitude.

Because before they were clients, they were neighbors.
And when people see that you care enough to celebrate them — they'll stay with you through anything.

Community Reputation and Online Presence

Your reputation is your shadow — it follows you everywhere, long after you leave the room.
In small towns, that shadow can stretch for miles.

People talk. They remember how you treated them when you didn't need something. They remember if you showed up when times got tough, or if you hid behind excuses.

Your name gets passed around faster than any business card — in the feed store, in the bleachers on Friday nights, in the local Facebook group where someone asks, "Who's a good insurance agent around here?"

If you've done your job right, your name doesn't just show up once.
It shows up *again and again*, backed by people who vouch for your character before they ever mention your pricing.

That's what reputation really is — **trust spoken out loud by other people.**

Be Seen Before You're Needed

The best kind of marketing happens before the sale.
Show up in your community before they ever think to call you.

That might mean:
• Sponsoring the local Little League team.
• Donating raffle items to the school fundraiser.
• Handing out cold water at a summer parade.
• Supporting the local FFA auction or youth programs.

Every small moment you show up tells the community who you
are and what you stand for. And when people *see* you enough,
they start to believe in you before they ever need your service.

Online Reputation — The New Town Square

The digital world is the new Main Street.
Your name now lives online — on Google reviews, social media,
and local group chats.

For years, I built my name the old-fashioned way: shaking hands,
sponsoring events, being visible. But today, I've seen the power
of both worlds working together.

When someone sees you at a community event *and* online the
next day, your credibility doubles.

I can't count the times I've opened Facebook and seen:
"Who should I call for insurance?"
…and then watched as multiple people tagged my name.

That's when you know your reputation is working for you —
even when you're not in the room.

Field Note: "Every post, handshake, and phone call adds up to a reputation. Guard it carefully — it speaks louder than any advertisement."

Keep Politics Out, Keep Service In

One rule I live by: never mix politics with professionalism.
You'll never win a client over a political post — but you can lose five because of one.

Your business page should be safe, kind, and professional.
Post helpful content, share tips, celebrate client wins, highlight your team — and stay true to your values without crossing into division.

People come to you for protection, not politics.
Keep your platform a place of trust and unity.

Handling Problems Before They Happen

Long-term clients don't stay because life is perfect.
They stay because they trust you'll help them through the imperfect moments.

That means being *proactive.*
When a carrier issue, billing error, or rate change happens, you can either hide from it or own it.

I've learned to call my clients first — *before* they ever open the letter or see the notice.

I'll say:

"Hey, I wanted to reach out before you get a letter in the mail. Rates went up this year — mine did too. Let's talk through your options and see if there's a better fit."
That call changes everything.

They don't feel blindsided. They feel protected.
And that builds trust that lasts decades.

The Power of Proactive Communication

The agents who win aren't the ones with the best marketing —
they're the ones who make the first call.

Proactive agents control the narrative.
Reactive agents chase it.

If something goes wrong, your silence speaks louder than any
apology. But when you show up early with empathy and a plan,
you turn frustration into gratitude — and gratitude into loyalty.

Real Life Example — The Phone Call That Prevented a Fire

Years ago, I noticed a carrier notice buried in my inbox about
upcoming auto rate changes. I could've ignored it, like many do,
and hoped nobody noticed. But something told me to call.

I started with one of my longest-term families. When I explained
the change before they got the letter, the husband paused and
said,

> "Steven, you're the only person who's ever called us before a
> rate increase."

They stayed. And because of that one call, so did their kids and
parents.
It wasn't the rate that kept them — it was the respect.

Field Note: "Clients don't expect perfection — they expect presence. The first call they get from you shouldn't be an apology. It should be a solution."

Building Trust in the Hard Moments

Trust isn't built during easy renewals or smooth claims.
It's built during the tough calls, the confusing letters, and the unexpected changes.

You can't script authenticity. People know when you're being real.
So be honest, even when it's uncomfortable.

The most loyal clients I've ever had weren't the ones where everything went perfectly.
They were the ones who saw me make things right when they didn't.

Creating Systems That Keep Clients

Talent will win you attention.
Charisma will win you a few deals.
But systems — reliable, repeatable systems — are what keep clients from walking out the same door they came in.

As your book grows, memory stops being enough. You can't track hundreds of renewals, birthdays, and policy details in your head. Systems make your care scalable. They make sure every client, from your first to your five-hundredth, feels remembered and respected.

My Retention Framework

Here's how I structure my agency so no client ever slips through the cracks:

- Renewal Alerts (60-30-15 rule) –
  Automated reminders fire at 60, 30, and 15 days before renewal so my team can review, call, and schedule check-ins early. Surprises kill trust; preparation builds it.
- Quarterly Touchpoints –
  Every client hears from us at least four times a year. Sometimes it's a handwritten note, sometimes a phone call, sometimes just a "thinking of you" text. Small gestures, big impact.
- Milestone Recognition –
  Birthdays, home closings, business anniversaries — they all matter. People remember the agent who remembers them.
- Referral Rhythm –
  At each major touchpoint, we gently remind clients that referrals are appreciated. It's never a sales ask; it's a thank-you opportunity.
- Annual Reviews –
  Once a year, we sit down — in person or virtually — to make sure coverage still fits life. It prevents surprises, protects families, and strengthens loyalty.

Each layer reinforces the next. Together, they form the safety net that keeps your retention high and your reputation stronger.

Technology That Supports — Not Replaces — Relationships

You don't need a fancy CRM to start.
Even a spreadsheet can serve as a reminder system if used consistently.

But once your agency scales, technology becomes your ally.
Automations handle the nudges so you can focus on the nuances.

- Automate reminders, not relationships.
- Use templates for consistency, but always personalize.
- Let technology catch the tasks — you catch the tone.

Real Life Example – Losing and Winning Through Systems

Early in my career, I lost a loyal client because I didn't call before renewal. They switched carriers after another agent reached out first. It wasn't about price or coverage — it was about presence.

That loss stung. But it pushed me to build my first reminder system.
Years later, a similar situation popped up — but this time, my system flagged it 30 days early. I called, reviewed the account, fixed a coverage gap, and not only kept the client, but gained their parents and two coworkers through referrals.

The difference wasn't talent.
It was timing.

Field Note: "Presence isn't an accident. It's a system disguised as care."

Making Retention Part of Your Agency Culture

Every team member should know: keeping a client is as valuable as landing one.
Retention isn't a back-office duty — it's a shared mindset.

Celebrate renewals like you celebrate new sales.
Reward team members who maintain high retention.
Track not just how much you write, but how much you keep.
When your agency values retention publicly, it becomes part of your identity.

The Compounding Power of Consistency

A single call or card won't build loyalty — but fifty will.
A single storm check-in won't define you — but the pattern of care will.

Each act may feel small, but together they create a reputation that money can't buy.
Consistency compounds.

Your reputation starts to travel without you — in local conversations, at the feed store, on social media, in church pews. People say your name before you ever meet them, and when they do, they already trust you.

That's when you know your business has crossed from hustle to heritage.

Lifetime Value — The Long Game

The greatest agents don't chase quick wins. They build lifetime value.
One young couple can turn into decades of business — from their first car to their retirement home, from their children's first car to their grandchildren's first policy.

Every renewal, every referral, every small act of care is a seed planted.
Over years, those seeds grow into an orchard that feeds not just your income, but your legacy.

That's how your business becomes generational.
That's how you eventually pass it to your children or a loyal team who carries your name forward with pride.

Final Thought: From Transactions to Legacy

In this chapter, we covered the quiet side of success — the side that doesn't make noise on leaderboards but echoes in loyalty for years.

Retention isn't glamorous, but it's golden.
It's what keeps your book strong when markets shift.
It's what builds stability when new leads slow.
It's what turns first-time clients into lifelong advocates.

Remember:

- Call before they call you.
- Be honest when rates rise.
- Check in when they least expect it.
- Celebrate, don't just sell.
- Keep politics out of business, and people at the center.
- Build systems that make kindness scalable.

Do these things and you'll look up one day to find something beautiful:
your clients didn't just buy policies — they built a life with you by their side.

That's not just retention.
That's reputation.
That's legacy.

"let us not become weary in doing good, for at the proper time we will reap a harvest if we do not give up."

- *Galatians 6:9*

Chapter 7: Beginning with Client Experience

The Client Experience Standard (SOP)

Because leadership is not just how you treat your team — it's how your team treats your clients.

One of the most important reflections I had when editing this chapter was this: I never explained how I expect clients to be treated inside my agency. You can build systems, recruit agents, and preach culture — but if a client walks through your doors and is met with indifference or chaos, everything else you built starts to crumble.

A great agency is not built on policies — it's built on experiences people never forget.

So in my office, client treatment is not left to chance. It is intentional, consistent, and expected from every team member.

The Wiatrek Group Client Experience Standard

(This is the exact system we train to — from the moment a client walks in, to the moment they leave.)

1. Arrival & Greeting (Front Desk SOP)

Goal: Make every client feel seen within the first 5 seconds.

- As soon as a client walks in, the receptionist or team member at the front must:
  - Make eye contact
  - Smile
  - Greet warmly

Required greeting script example:
"Hi there! Welcome to Wiatrek Group — who can we get you taken care of with today?"

- The receptionist immediately phones the agent or walks to notify them in person — no exceptions.
- If the agent can't be at the front within 60–90 seconds, the receptionist must say:
  "Steven is just wrapping up and will be with you shortly — can I get you water or coffee while you wait?"

2. Agent Greeting & Escort to Office

When the agent arrives at the front:

- Must greet with a handshake, eye contact, and smile
- Use the client's name if possible

Example:
"Mr. Johnson! Good to see you. Thanks for coming in — come on back and we'll get you taken care of."

- The agent walks with the client — never pointing or yelling, "My office is down there."

3. Inside the Office — Privacy & Professionalism Protocol

Once seated in the office:
- Close the door — every single time — to provide privacy.
- Place cell phone inside the drawer — not face-down on the desk.
- Set desk phone or soft-phone to Do Not Disturb.
- Computer notifications silenced.
- No personal conversations, side chatter, or interruptions once meeting begins.

This signals to the client: You have 100% of my attention.

4. Conversation Flow (The Meeting Structure)

Warm Open (Always ask before quoting anything):

"Before we dive into your policy — has anything changed? Vehicles, drivers, home upgrades, business changes, or life events I should know about?"

Purpose & Process (Sets expectations upfront):

"So here's the plan — we'll review what you have, identify any gaps or overlaps, compare better options if they exist, and I'll make sure you know exactly what your coverage does and doesn't do. Sound fair?"

During the Appointment:

- Listen more than you speak
- Avoid insurance jargon unless explained in plain English
- Take notes — but not while the client is sharing something personal or emotional
- Never multitask on emails or side work during a client meeting

5. Closing the Appointment & Next Steps

Before the client leaves the office:
- Summarize what was discussed
- Give clear next actions (who is doing what and by when)
- Ask if they have any remaining questions

Example Script:
"So just to confirm — I'll run the updated home and auto quotes with the roof discount and higher liability. You'll have that by tomorrow at 3 p.m. If anything changes, I'll call you sooner. Does that sound good?"

6. Escort & Exit — The Rule Most Agencies Skip (But We Don't)

Once the meeting is finished:
- The agent must walk the client back to the front desk — not let them find their own way out.
- Shake their hand again and thank them.

Script example:
"I appreciate you coming in today. Thank you for taking the time to visit — I'll be in touch by tomorrow. Have a great rest of your day."

7. After the Client Leaves

- Notes from the meeting must be entered into the CRM the same day
- Any follow-up task is scheduled with a hard deadline (not just "I'll get to it")
- If a quote or promise was made — it must be delivered within 24 business hours or earlier
- If a claim was discussed — a follow-up call or text occurs within 24 hours

8. Claims & Emergency Situations

If a client walks in or calls in panic:

- Everything pauses. Service takes priority over sales.
- Bring them into a private office immediately.
- Guide them step-by-step through filing the claim or contacting the carrier.
- Document everything — and follow up the next day.

Why This Matters

Because people don't remember premiums.
They remember how you made them feel.

Because loyalty isn't built through price — it's built through trust, professionalism, and consistency.

Because leadership isn't what you say — it's what your team repeatedly does when you're not around.

Leadership vs. Management

Leadership inspires.
Management controls.
Both are important — but they are not the same.

Management is about processes, checklists, compliance, and making sure the trains run on time. Leadership is about vision, trust, and helping people become more than they believed they could be.

A manager asks, "Did you do the task?"
A leader asks, "Do you understand the purpose behind the task — and how can I help you get better?"

A manager uses authority.
A leader uses influence.

A manager focuses on policies.
A leader focuses on people.

Micromanagement Kills Momentum

One of the biggest mistakes new agency owners make is thinking leadership means control. They hover, they nitpick, they demand updates every hour, and they unintentionally smother creativity and confidence.

Micromanagement:
- Creates anxiety
- Destroys initiative
- Makes people operate out of fear, not ownership
- Builds dependency instead of leaders

People don't grow when every move is dictated. They grow when they are trusted, equipped, and held accountable to rise on their own.

How I Lead My Team (Not Manage Them)

My own team jokes and calls me a "flinging shopkeeper" — because I give them enough rope to climb or enough rope to hang themselves. And they're not wrong.

Here's how I approach leadership:

- I train with them.
- I ride along with them.
- I answer the phone at 8 PM when they're stuck.
- But I do not babysit them.

We don't have corporate quotas or dashboards hanging over their head each morning. But we do have expectations.

My core leadership principles:
- I give them the tools
- I show them the example
- I tell them the truth — even when it hurts
- Then I let them build their success

There's no hand-holding. No begging. No chasing.

Accountability with Freedom

My team is 100% commission-based — no salary, no safety net. That alone creates responsibility. But I add one more layer:

- Every agent pays a $150 "membership fee" each month
- It covers their CRM seat, automation tools, e-sign software, and systems
- I don't charge for desk space — I charge for their tools and opportunity

Why?

Because when people invest—even a little—they take their career seriously.

They show up.
They prospect harder.
They quit making excuses.

The first time someone doesn't write business and still owes me $150, it becomes very real for them.

Motivation Through Example

Each month, I tell my team:

"Whoever outsells me this month gets their $150 fee paid back by me."

So far, I haven't lost.
I'm always the first one in the office. More often than not, I'm the last one to leave. I don't ask my agents to do anything I'm not willing to do myself.

Because leadership isn't about standing in front — it's about being the standard.

One Final Thought on Leadership vs. Management

You can manage tasks.
You can systemize processes.
You can automate emails.

But you can only lead people.
People don't follow your title.
They follow your example, your integrity, and your belief in them.

Creating a Culture of Abundance & Collaboration

One of the biggest challenges in building an agency isn't sales, marketing, or even hiring. It's culture. Not the fake "mission statements on the wall" kind—but the real kind you feel the second you walk into the office.

Culture is built in everyday habits:

- How your team talks about clients
- How they treat each other when you're not in the room
- How they respond when someone succeeds
- How they behave when nobody is watching

A great agency culture doesn't happen by accident. It is taught, demonstrated, protected, and repeated—over and over again.

Scarcity vs. Abundance

I tell my team early and often:

"There are two ways to live in business—through scarcity or abundance."

Scarcity mindset sounds like:

- "There are only so many clients."
- "If someone else wins, I lose."
- "Protect your leads, don't share anything."
- "Keep your secrets—don't help your competition."

Abundance mindset sounds like:

- "There's more than enough business for everyone."
- "When someone wins, it proves what's possible."
- "We don't guard information—we multiply it."
- "When we help others, we grow faster."

Scarcity creates jealousy, office gossip, and quiet resentment. Abundance creates collaboration, loyalty, innovation, and energy.

We Are Not Employees — We Are Business Owners

From day one, I tell every new agent:
"You are now a business owner who happens to sell insurance."

You don't work for me.
You work with me.
You work for your last name.
You work for your family and your legacy.

This shift in mindset changes everything:

- You stop clocking in—you start building up.
- You stop asking "what's my commission?" and start asking "how big can my book grow?"
- You stop feeling threatened by others—and start growing with them.

Internal Collaboration (Team Helping Team)

In our agency:

- Top producers openly share what scripts worked for them.
- New agents ask for help—and receive it without judgment.
- Each week, one agent teaches a short training on something that worked for them ("What helped me close two deals this week…").
- If one person is in a slump—we don't mock them—we help them.

External Collaboration (Even With Competitors)

This surprises most people—but I even encourage my agents to build friendships with other insurance agents in town, including competitors.

Why?

Because:

- When you can't place a risk, you can refer it to someone who can (and vice versa).
- When disasters hit—wildfires, hailstorms, tornados—everyone helps each other.
- Your reputation in your community becomes stronger than any advertisement.

A rising tide lifts all ships.
When you stop fighting for scraps and start playing the long game—doors open.

Culture is Not What You Preach — It's What You Protect

Culture is not built by posters on a wall or slogans in a meeting. It is built by the behaviors you allow or refuse to allow.

In my agency:

- Gossip is not tolerated. You talk to people, not about them.
- We celebrate wins publicly and coach weaknesses privately.
- Backstabbing, drama, and silent resentment are addressed quickly and directly.
- We don't compete against each other—we compete against who we were last month.

Final Thought on Culture & Abundance

People don't leave agencies because of commission percentages—they leave because of culture.

They will stay for:
- Respect
- Belonging
- Growth
- Shared purpose
- The feeling of being part of something bigger than themselves

You can teach someone how to sell insurance.
You cannot teach someone to stay loyal to something they don't believe in.

So build something worth believing in.

Culture Is Your Secret Weapon

Faith. Family. Community.

You can't buy culture.
You can't fake it.
You can only live it, protect it, and pass it on.

Most agency owners focus on numbers—premium, policies, revenue. Those matter. But what truly separates an average agency from a legacy agency isn't sales—it's culture.
People don't stay because of contracts.
They stay because of connection.

And in my agency, our culture is built on three pillars:

1. Faith – The Foundation of Service

Faith, for me, is not a marketing tactic or a decorative quotation in the lobby. It is the belief that we are called to serve people with compassion, honesty, and humility.

Faith shows up in small ways:

- When a widow sits in our office, overwhelmed after losing her husband—we don't rush through paperwork. We sit. We listen. Sometimes we pray with her. Sometimes we just stay silent with her.
- When a family files a devastating claim—our first response isn't, "Let me get the carrier on the line." It's, "Are you okay? Do you need a place to stay tonight? Has anyone brought you food yet?"

We may sell insurance, but often what we really provide is peace, compassion, and presence.

2. Family – Why We Work the Way We Do

very agent knows it—we don't work these hours, make these calls, or endure rejection for fun.
We do it for our families.
But in leadership, the definition of family grows. The bigger your agency becomes, the more people your decisions affect—not just your household, but the households of your team.

Every policy written…
Every claim paid…
Every renewal protected…
…is someone's family, protected because of the work we do.

So in my agency:

- We celebrate marriages, babies, graduations, and victories.
- When someone struggles—we stand with them.
- When someone achieves something great—we cheer, loudly.
- When someone's kid has a game—we let them leave early and go. Business will wait. Family won't.

3. Community – The Cord That Binds Us

One thread is easy to snap.
A cord of three strands—faith, family, and community—is not easily broken.

Our agency does not exist just to write policies. We exist to serve the town that raised us, trusted us, and gave us a name.
So we:

- Sponsor local baseball teams and 4-H kids
- Support school fundraisers and FFA auctions
- Volunteer at festivals and charity events
- Show up at funerals, weddings, and town hall meetings
- Stay visible—not just on billboards, but in person

Because when you show up for your community—
your community shows up for you.

Culture Isn't Written — It's Lived

Culture is not a paragraph in an employee handbook.
It is the way:

- Your secretary greets people on a Monday morning
- Your agents speak about clients behind closed doors
- You treat your team when numbers are low
- You handle mistakes—not with fear, but with accountability and growth
- You respond when nobody is watching

The Result of Culture Done Right

When you build a culture rooted in faith, family, and community:
- Clients stop price shopping — they stay because they feel valued
- Agents stop leaving — because they don't just have a job, they have a home
- People don't come to work just to make a living — they come to make a difference

That's what makes culture your unbeatable, uncopiable advantage.
Anyone can copy your pricing.
They can copy your website.
They may even copy your scripts.
But they can't copy your heart.

Compensation & Motivation

Fair Pay, Real Ownership, and the Psychology Behind Why People Stay

Money matters — but it's not what keeps people loyal.

People will show up for a paycheck.
But they will go to war for a leader who believes in them, pays them fairly, and treats them like partners instead of employees.

That's why compensation inside my agency isn't built on pressure or manipulation — it's built on ownership.

My Compensation Philosoph

Pay people well. Trust them deeply. Expect them to earn it.

Most agency owners hold onto the biggest piece of the pie and throw agents whatever crumbs are left. That may work short-term — but it destroys loyalty, motivation, and longevity.

So I flipped the script.

- My agency keeps 15% of the commission.
- The producer keeps 85%, on both new and renewal business.
- No back-end gimmicks. No fine print. No games.

Why? Because I know what it feels like to start over — with a family to feed and a bank account nearly empty. I don't ever want my agents to feel like I withheld opportunity from them.

Why I Pay the Lion's Share:

- Fairness breeds loyalty – People don't leave when they're respected and rewarded.
- Ownership mindset – When agents take home most of the revenue, they start acting like business owners.
- Recruiting advantage – Talented agents leave greedy agencies and join mine.
- Retention advantage – Well-paid producers stay, build bigger books, and treat clients better.

Why I Don't Use Bonus Games or Empty Incentives

I don't dangle gift cards, TVs, or "bonus trips you may or may not qualify for."

I don't pay $200 per life policy, or $100 per umbrella, or $50 per cross-sell.
Why? Because those systems teach agents to chase trinkets — not build legacies.

Instead:
- I pay everything honestly, upfront, every time.
- Their income is 100% tied to their effort, relationships, and consistency.
- That's how you build business owners — not order takers.

The Accountability System: Skin in the Game

Every agent pays a $150 per month membership fee.

This isn't rent.
It isn't a penalty.
It covers:
- CRM Seat
- E-Signature Platform
- Automation Software
- Marketing Tools
- Client Portals

The message is simple:

"I don't charge you for a desk. I charge you for tools. This
    business can make you wealthy — but you must invest in it."

And it works.
The first time an agent earns $0 but still owes me $150, they
quickly learn that effort matters and success is not handed out —
it's earned.

The Competition That Keeps Things Fun

Every month I tell my team:

"If you outsell me this month, I'll pay your $150 for you."

I've yet to pay it.

Not because they can't — but because they know I'm in the
trenches too.

I'm the first one in the office.
Often the last one to leave.

They see me writing policies, answering phones, making cold calls, and sitting with clients.

And because of that — they don't just hear about work ethic — they witness it.

Recognition That Actually Matters

Money motivates — but recognition multiplies.

Inside my agency, we recognize:

- First policy ever written
- First life insurance sale
- First 100 policies
- First $50,000 month
- Acts of service (claim handled well, client prayed for, widow comforted, volunteer work done)
- Reviews earned from clients by name

We ring bells, give high-fives, and celebrate small wins — because small wins, stacked over time, create careers.

Turnover vs Stability: The Math Nobody Talks About

Bad agencies think they save money by paying low splits. What they don't calculate is the hidden cost of losing good people:

Cost of Losing an Agent	Impact
Lost renewals	6-12 months of premium gone
Lost relationships	Clients follow the agent
Time to train replacement	3-6 months
Lost referrals	Families stop sending business
Damage to culture	Morale drops

A generous commission structure with high retention always outperforms a stingy one with constant turnover. Always.

Bottom Line:

You don't keep people by paying them the least you can get away with.
You keep people by paying them so well they'd feel foolish leaving—
and by treating them so well they'd feel guilty abandoning the mission.

Retention & Development of Your Team

Recruiting brings them in. Leadership makes them stay.

Most agency owners think their biggest challenge is recruiting agents. It's not.

The biggest challenge is keeping good agents, growing them, and turning them into future leaders. People don't leave because of money — they leave because they don't feel supported, developed, or believed in.

A paycheck can buy time.
But it cannot buy loyalty.
Loyalty comes from trust, mentorship, development, and shared vision.

Why Most Agents Leave Agencies

It's rarely about commission. It's usually because they feel:

- Alone
- Unappreciated
- Micromanaged
- Untrained and overwhelmed
- Or worst of all — like just another number

People don't quit jobs.
They quit leaders who stop leading them.

How I Build Retention Into My Agency

I decided early on:
If I'm going to recruit someone into this business — especially someone with a family — then I owe it to them to be present, honest, and available.

So here's what I do:

1. Monthly Team Check-Ins

Every month, we sit down as a team — not to lecture, but to align.

We:

- Review our premium goals
- Celebrate wins (big or small)
- Discuss where we can grow
- Share any struggles (without judgment or blame)
- Commit to action steps for the next 30 days

It's not corporate. There are no slide decks or quotas being thrown at anyone. It's real talk around a table.

2. Open-Door Mentorship

My agents know:
Insurance doesn't stop at 5 p.m. — and neither do I.

If they're stuck on a quote at 8:30 at night, I answer.
If they're nervous before a big commercial presentation, I ride along.
If they fail, I don't shame them — I help them rebuild.

Not because I have to — but because someone did that for me.

3. Transparency Creates Trust

Every month I show my agents exactly how they're paid and how much I'm keeping.

Why?

Because when people see fairness...
They stop acting like employees.
They start acting like owners.

And owners don't quietly wait for instructions. They move.

4. Servant Leadership (How I Learned It)

When I was a young captive agent, I had a mentor named Mark.

He once told me, "If your truck ever breaks down or you ever get stuck — call me. I'll come get you."

I didn't think he meant it—until my truck wouldn't start one icy morning at 5:45 a.m. I had appointments scheduled. I called him. He answered the phone half-asleep, said "Where are you?" and 20 minutes later, he pulled into my driveway.

No paycheck can buy that kind of leadership.
It's earned through presence, reliability, and action.

Now, every time I answer my phone late at night, or drive across town to help a new agent, I think of Mark.

Retention Is Earned — Not Demanded

Here's the truth:

You can't force loyalty.
You can't demand passion.
You can't mandate belief.
You must build it, earn it, and model it.
Retention happens naturally when:
- People feel seen and supported
- They are paid fairly and trained well
- Their leader fights with them, not against them
- They believe they're part of something bigger than themselves

Final Thoughts: Legacy Leadership

Leadership is not about titles or offices or override checks.

Leadership is a calling.

It's the quiet shift from success to significance — from "How much can I earn?" to "How many people can I grow?"

Your agency will not be remembered for how many policies you sold...
But for how many people you lifted.

Og Mandino said it best:

"Tomorrow is the day when the weak become strong."

Your job is to believe in others until they believe in themselves.

Build your agency with:

- Vision
- Systems
- Standards
- Faith
- Compassion
- Service

And one day — you will look around and realize this agency is no longer just a business.
It's a family.
It's a legacy.
It's proof that leadership, done right, multiplies beyond you.

"The measure of a life is not what we gather, but what we give."
　　　　　　-　*Unknown*

Conclusion

When I walked away from my captive agency after ten and a half years, I didn't feel victorious—I felt hollow. For more than a decade, I had built my identity around being "the XYZ Company guy." I had built relationships, a name in my community, and a personal brand that I thought would be with me forever. Overnight, that identity disappeared.

My income was zero. My confidence was cracked. I was no longer the man people recognized by company logo, but a man standing in front of an uncertain future.

That moment was one of the darkest seasons of my life. It wasn't just the loss of a job or a title. It was the loss of identity, purpose, and direction. After 10.5 years of building a name, I found myself having to start over with nothing but my name and my grit.
But in that darkness, I realized something profound: we all have choices in life. We can be victims of our circumstances, or we can take accountability for our future.

I made the decision to rise.

Starting over wasn't easy. There were days when doubt was louder than determination. There were nights when the thought of giving up felt tempting. But every time I sat in silence, I reminded myself of something simple and powerful:

I've spent over a decade helping other people build trust, build protection, build their dreams. If I could do that for others, why couldn't I do it for myself?

So I opened my own agency with no marketing budget, no corporate backing, no fancy tech stack. Just a belief that the same old-school principles that built my first book of business would build this new chapter too.

I leaned on the power of handshakes, kitchen table meetings, and genuine conversations. I didn't chase cold leads or buy overpriced lists. I invested my time where it mattered most—people.

In less than a year, this approach built a book of 70 clients and $350,000 in premium. I hired two part-time producers, and I'm in the process of adding one full-time producer. I didn't spend a dime on marketing because my community, my relationships, and my work ethic became the marketing.

And when I think about that first year, what stands out isn't the numbers themselves—it's the fact that they are proof of concept.

- Proof that old-school, relationship-driven selling still works in a digital world.
- Proof that a personal connection can outlast algorithms and auto-dialers.
- Proof that a kitchen table and a handshake can still build a business.

I don't say this to boast. I say this to show what's possible.

Eight months before that milestone, I was in a place of doubt, fear, and frustration. Today, I stand as an agency owner with a vision, a team, and a future.

This book is not a corporate sales manual. It's not a list of gimmicks or scripts. It's a story of starting over, of betting on yourself, and of choosing to lead with authenticity.

It's my blueprint. But more importantly—it can be yours too.

If you're reading this and you're in a place where your confidence has been shaken… or maybe your career feels stuck—let me tell you something: I know exactly what that feels like.

I know what it's like to stare at a blank page and wonder if everything you built was for nothing. But I also know what it feels like to take that first shaky step forward... then another... and another... until one day you realize you've built something stronger than what you lost.

Your journey may not look exactly like mine. You may have your own doubts, your own fears, and your own path to carve. But the principles are universal:

- Trust matters.
- Relationships matter.
- Showing up matters.

If you commit to these things—not for a week or a month—but consistently over time, your life and your business will change.

Remember this: you are not your company name. You are not your title. You are the value you bring to others.

When I lost the logo that defined me for over a decade, I learned that my true value wasn't in a brand—it was in how I treated people, how I built trust, and how I showed up every day.

If I could go back and talk to the version of me that was sitting in that dark place after leaving captive, I'd tell him:

"This isn't the end. It's the beginning. Your identity isn't gone—it's just no longer borrowed."

Maybe that's what you need to hear too.

Maybe today is your beginning.

So I want to challenge you:
Don't just close this book and move on. Take a deep breath and make a decision.

- Decide to take ownership of your story.
- Decide to bet on yourself.
- Decide that you are worth more than someone else's opinion of your value.

If you've been labeled as burned out, irrelevant, or stuck—use it as fuel.

If you've been overlooked or underestimated—let it sharpen your focus.

If you've been afraid to start again—take this as proof that you can.

This industry doesn't belong to just the fastest talkers or the biggest advertisers. It belongs to those who build trust, serve their communities, and show up with integrity.

It belongs to people like you—if you choose to claim it.

So shake that hand.
Make that call.
Knock on that door.
Show up for people.

Build something real.

Build something that no one can take from you.

Build something that reflects who you are, not just what you sell.
This isn't just about insurance. It's about legacy.

It's about proving to yourself that your story still matters.
It's about creating something that lasts beyond quotas, beyond contracts, beyond titles.

Less than a year after I walked away from everything I knew, I built a new identity, a new agency, and a new purpose.

And if I can do it—so can you.

Your story isn't over.

It's just waiting for the chapter you're about to write.
This is your time to elevate.

Closing Invitation

If this book has helped you in any way—whether it inspired you to pick up the phone, rebuild your confidence, or start fresh in your career—I'd love to hear from you.

Share your story. Tag me on LinkedIn: (www.linkedin.com/in/steven-wiatrek-a96492125)

Let me celebrate your success right alongside you.

You never know who your story might inspire next.

And if you're willing, send me a picture and a short note about how this book made a difference in your career. Who knows— your story might be the one I share next to encourage another agent to keep going when times get tough.

Epilogue

When I look back on the road that led me here, I can't help but see every struggle, setback, and moment of doubt as part of something much greater. I once thought that success was a finish line—something you reached and held onto. But I've come to understand that true success is not a destination at all; it's a continual awakening of purpose.

There was a time when I questioned everything—when the future seemed foggy and the past felt heavier than my dreams. But through it all, I discovered that the fire inside me was not extinguished; it was being refined. The trials that once broke me now serve as the forge that remade me. I am not the same man who began this journey. I am stronger, sharper, and infinitely more aware of who I am and what I am called to do.

I write these final words not as a man seeking sympathy, but as one who has found strength through surrender. I have learned that we are never truly alone when we walk with purpose. The world will always whisper doubts, but you must learn to listen instead to the quiet certainty of your own heart. For it is in that still voice that greatness is born.

To those standing where I once stood—uncertain, overwhelmed, or questioning if you still have what it takes—remember this: the world does not reward those who wait for perfect moments. It rewards those who dare to move forward despite their fears. You do not need permission to chase your destiny; you only need the courage to take the first step.

I have walked through the fire and emerged reforged. I am no longer bound by the expectations of others or the fear of failure. I am my own master—guided by faith, integrity, and a relentless desire to serve. I do not apologize for dreaming big, nor do I hide from the world's opinion. I have learned to stand tall in both success and struggle, because both have made me who I am.

To the reader holding this book: may it remind you that you, too, have a fire within that cannot be extinguished by doubt or defeat. Your story is still being written. And when the world tries to tell you to give up, smile quietly to yourself and remember: iron sharpens iron, and your moment to rise will come.

So, my friend—lift your head, take a deep breath, and step boldly into the future. You've already survived the worst. Now go create your best. The world needs more dreamers who dare to do.

Invite Steven Wiatrek to Speak

If this book inspired you or your team and you'd like me to share these lessons in person, I'd be honored to speak at your next event. Whether it's an agency meeting, corporate leadership retreat, or industry conference, I focus on helping agents reignite purpose, sharpen skills, and build businesses that last.

My sessions aren't lectures—they're conversations. Real stories. Real lessons. Real results. I teach from the same heart that built this book: practical, personal, and proven.

Topics Include:

- Purpose-driven sales and service
- Old-school fundamentals that still win
- Rebuilding after setbacks (resilience and leadership)
- Community, legacy, and client loyalty

Universities & Community Colleges
I speak at no charge for universities and community colleges—all I ask is that travel is covered and books are purchased for students.

Bookings & Bulk Orders
To discuss speaking opportunities, collaborations, or bulk book orders, contact me at:
LinkedIn: linkedin.com/in/steven-wiatrek-a96492125
Email: swiatrek@gmail.com

Let's continue building a stronger, more inspired community of agents—one meeting, one story, and one success at a time.

"A single voice can ignite a spark, but a united message can light the world.